1 MONTH OF
FREE
READING

at

www.ForgottenBooks.com

By purchasing this book you are eligible for one month membership to ForgottenBooks.com, giving you unlimited access to our entire collection of over 1,000,000 titles via our web site and mobile apps.

To claim your free month visit:

www.forgottenbooks.com/free790501

ISBN 978-0-483-59500-2
PIBN 10790501

THE GLORY OF GOD IS INTELLIGENCE.

VOL. V. AUGUST, 1884 No. 11.

THE

CONTRIBUTOR

A MONTHLY MAGAZINE OF HOME LITERATURE.

REPRESENTS THE

YOUNG ✦ MEN'S ✦ AND ✦ YOUNG ✦ LADIES' ✦ MUTUAL ✦ IMPROVEMENT ✦ ASSOCIATIONS ✦ OF ✦ THE ✦ LATTER - DAY ✦ SAINTS.

EDITED AND PUBLISHED BY JUNIUS F. WELLS

SALT LAKE CITY, UTAH.

THE CONTRIBUTOR.

CONTENTS FOR AUGUST, 1884.

THE CONTRIBUTOR.

The Glory of God is Intelligence.

VOL. V.   AUGUST, 1884.   No. 11.

HISTORY OF THE BOOK OF MORMON.

TRANSLATION OF THE RECORDS.—II.

SINCE writing the preceding chapter the following detailed description of the manuscript in the hands of David Whitmer has been published by the Lamoni (Iowa) *Herald*, the organ of the Reorganized (Josephite) Church:

"With but one or two exceptions, proper names begin with capitals, and the capital I is always written for the pronoun I; and sentences are generally begun with capitals, when they do not begin with the character &. The lines were closely and finely written, and from edge to edge of the sheets. The paper was evidently ruled by hand. The pages contained about thirty-eight lines each, and average fourteen words to a line, or over two hundred and forty-six thousand words in the manuscript. The writing was very legible, and the manuscript was well preserved. It measures about one and one-half inches thick, eight inches wide, and thirteen inches long; four hundred and sixty-four pages, exclusive of preface and testimonials. The word 'and' is nearly always represented by the character '&.' "

TESTIMONY OF THE THREE WITNESSES.

It now becomes our pleasing duty to investigate that very interesting and important incident in the translation of the Book of Mormon—the revelation of the plates to the three special witnesses whose testimony prefaces that holy record. The names of these witnesses are Oliver Cowdery, David Whitmer and Martin Harris. We will first introduce the Prophet Joseph's account of the matter, and afterwards append some of the testimonies of those most interested. In the "History of Joseph Smith" it is written:

"In the course of the work of translation, we ascertained that three special witnesses were to be provided by the Lord, to whom he would grant that they should see the plates from which this work (the Book of Mormon) should be translated, and that these three witnesses should bear record of the same, as will be found recorded, Book of Mormon first edition, page ——, and second edition, page ——.

"Almost immediately after we had made this discovery, it occurred to Oliver Cowdery, David Whitmer and the afore-mentioned Martin Harris (who had come to enquire after our progress in the work) that they would have me enquire of the Lord to know if they might not obtain of Him to be these three special witnesses, and finally they became so very solicitous, and teased me so much, that at length I complied, and through the Urim and Thummim I obtained of the Lord for them the following revelation:

"'Revelation to Oliver Cowdery, David Whitmer and Martin Harris at Fayette, Seneca County, New York, june, 1829, given previous to their viewing the plates containing the Book of Mormon.

"Behold, I say unto you, that you must rely upon my word, which if you do with full purpose of heart, you shall have a view of the plates, and also the breastplate, the sword of Laban, the Urim and Thummim, which were given to the brother of jared upon the mount when he talked with the Lord face to face, and the miraculous directors which were given to Lehi while in the wilderness, on the borders of the Red Sea; and it is by your faith that you shall obtain a view of them, even by that faith which was had by the prophets of old.

"And after that you have obtained faith, and have seen them with your eyes, you shall testify of them by the power of God, and this you shall do that my servant Joseph Smith, Jun., may not be destroyed, that I may bring about my righteous purposes unto the children of men in this work. And ye shall testify that you have seen them, even as my servant Joseph Smith, Jun., has seen them; for it is by my power that he has seen them, and it is because he had faith; and he has translated the book, even that part which I have commanded him; and as your Lord and your God liveth, it is true.

"Wherefore, you have received the same power, and the same faith, and the same gift like unto him; and if you do these last commandments of mine which I have given you, the gates of hell shall not prevail against you, for my grace is sufficient for you, and you shall be lifted up at the last day. And I, Jesus Christ, your Lord and your God, have spoken it unto you, that I might bring about my righteous purposes unto the children of men. Amen.

"Not many days after the above commandment was given, we four, viz., Martin Harris, David Whitmer, Oliver Cowdery and myself, agreed to retire into the woods, and try to obtain by fervent and humble prayer, the fulfilment of the promises given in the revelation, that they should have a view of the plates, etc. We accordingly made choice of a piece of woods convenient to Mr. Whitmer's house, to which we retired, and having knelt down we began to pray in much faith to Almighty God to bestow upon us a realization of these promises. According to previous arrangements, I commenced by vocal prayer to our heavenly Father, and was followed by each of the rest in succession. We did not, however, obtain

any answer or manifestation of the divine favor in our behalf. We again observed the same order of prayer, each calling on and praying fervently to God in rotation, but with the same result as before. Upon this our second failure, Martin Harris proposed that he should withdraw himself from us, believing, as he expressed himself, that his presence was the cause of our not obtaining what we wished for; he accordingly withdrew from us, and we knelt down again, and had not been many minutes engaged in prayer, when presently we beheld a light above us in the air of exceeding brightness; and, behold, an angel stood before us; in his hands he held the plates which we had been praying for these to have a view of; he turned over the leaves one by one, so that we could see them and discover the engravings thereon distinctly. He then addressed himself to David Whitmer, and said, 'David, blessed is the Lord, and he that keeps His commandments.' When immediately afterwards, we heard a voice from out of the bright light above us, saying, 'These plates have been revealed by the power of God, and they have been translated by the power of God. The translation of them which you have seen is correct, and I command you to bear record of what you now see and hear.'

"I now left David and Oliver, and went in pursuit of Martin Harris, whom I found at a considerable distance fervently engaged in prayer. He soon told me, however, that he had not yet prevailed with the Lord, and earnestly requested me to join him in prayer, that he also might realize the same blessings which we had just received. We accordingly joined in prayer, and ultimately obtained our desires, for before we had yet finished, the same vision was opened to our view, at least it was again to me, and I once more beheld and heard the same things, whilst at the same moment Martin Harris cried out, apparently in ecstacy of joy, ''Tis enough; mine eyes have beheld,' and jumping up, he shouted hosannah, blessing God, and otherwise rejoiced exceedingly.

"Having thus, through the mercy of God, obtained these manifestations, it now remained for these three individuals to fulfil the commandment which they had received, viz., to bear record of these things, in order to accomplish which they drew up and subscribed the following document."

Then follows the testimony of the three witnesses which we have already inserted.

In the year 1878, Elders Orson Pratt and Joseph F. Smith visited David Whitmer at his residence in Richmond, Missouri. After their interview (which occurred on the 7th of September), they made a report of its results to President Taylor and the Council of the Apostles; from this report we make the following exceedingly interesting extracts which form part of a conversation in which David Whitmer and his two distinguished visitors were the chief participants:

"Elder O. Pratt to D. Whitmer.—Can you tell the date of the bestowal of the Apostleship upon Joseph, by Peter, James and John?

"D. W.—I do not know, Joseph never told me. I can only tell you what I know, for I will not testify to anything I do not know.

"J. F. S. to D.W.—Did Oliver Cowdery die here in Richmond?

"D. W.—Yes, he lived here, I think, about one year before his death. He died in my father's house, right here, in January, 1849. Phineas Young was here at the time.

Elder O. P.—Do you remember what time you saw the plates?

"D. W.—It was in June, 1829—the latter part of the month, and the eight witnesses saw them, I think, the next day or the day after (*i. e.* one or two days after). Joseph showed them the plates himself, but the angel showed us (the three witnesses) the plates, as I suppose to fulfil the words of the book itself. Martin Harris was not with us at this time; he obtained a view of them afterwards (the same day). Joseph, Oliver and myself were together when I saw them. We not only saw the plates of the Book of Mormon but also the brass plates, the plates of the Book of Ether, the plates containing the records of the wickedness and secret combinations of the people of the world down to the time of their being engraved, and many other plates. The fact is, it was just as though Joseph, Oliver and I were sitting just here on a log, when we were overshadowed by a light. It was not like the light of the sun nor like that of a fire, but more glorious and beautiful. It extended away round us, I cannot tell how far, but in the midst of this light about as far off as he sits (pointing to John C. Whitmer, sitting a few feet from him), there appeared as it were, a table with many records or plates upon it, besides the plates of the Book of Mormon, also the sword of Laban, the directors—*i. e.*, the ball which Lehi had, and the Interpreters. I saw them just as plain as I see this bed (striking the bed beside him with his hand), and I heard the voice of the Lord, as distinctly as I ever heard anything in my life, declaring that the records of the plates of the Book of Mormon were translated by the gift and power of God.

"Elder O. P.—Did you see the angel at this time?

"D. W.—Yes, he stood before us. Our testimony as recorded in the Book of Mormon is strictly and absolutely true, just as it is there written. Before I ·knew Joseph, I had heard about him and the plates from persons who declared they knew he had them, and swore they would get them from him. When Oliver Cowdery went to Pennsylvania, he promised to write me what he should learn about these matters, which he did. He wrote me that Joseph had told him his (Oliver's) secret thoughts, and all he had meditated about going to see him, which no man on earth knew, as he supposed, but himself, and so he stopped to write for Joseph. Soon after this, Joseph sent for me (D. W.) to come to Harmony to get him and Oliver and bring them to my father's house. I did not know what to do, I was pressed with my work. I had some twenty acres to plow, so I concluded I would finish plowing and then go. I got up one morning to go to work as usual, and on going to the field, found between five and seven acres of my ground had been plowed during the night. I dou't know who did it; but it was done just as I would have done it myself, and the plow was left standing in the furrow. This enabled me to start sooner. When I arrived at Harmony, Joseph and Oliver were coming toward me, and met me some distance from the house. Oliver told me that Joseph had informed him when I started from home, where I had stopped the first night, how I read the sign at the tavern, where I stopped the next night, etc., and that I would be there that day before dinner, and this was why they had come out to meet me; all of which was exactly as Joseph had told Oliver, at which I was greatly astonished. When I was returning to Fayette, with Joseph and Oliver, all of us riding in the wagon, Oliver and I on an oldfashioned wooden spring seat and Joseph behind us; while traveling along in a clear open place, a very pleasant, nice-looking old man suddenly appeared by the side of our wagon and saluted us with 'good morning, it is very warm,' at the same time wiping his face or forehead with his hand. We returned the salutation, and, by a sign from Joseph, I invited him to ride if he was going our way. But he said very pleasantly, 'No, I am going to Cumorah.' This name was something new to me, I did not know what Cumorah meant. We all gazed at him and at each other, and as I looked around enquiringly of Joseph, the old man instantly disappeared, so that I did not see him again.

"J. F. S.—Did you notice his appearance?

"D. W.—I should think I did. He was, I should think, about five feet eight or nine inches tall and heavy set, about such a man as James Vancleave there, but heavier; his face was as large, he was dressed in a suit of brown woolen clothes, his hair and beard were white, like Brother Pratt's, but his beard was not so heavy. I also remember that he had on his back a sort of knapsack with something in, shaped like a book. It

was the messenger who had the plates, who had taken them from Joseph just prior to our starting from Harmony. Soon after our arrival home, I saw something which led me to the belief that the plates were placed or concealed in my father's barn. I frankly asked Joseph if my supposition was right, and he told me it was. Sometime after this, my mother was going to milk the cows, when she was met out near the yard by the same old man (judging by her description of him) who said to her: 'You have been very faithful and diligent in your labors, but you are tired because of the increase of your toil; it is proper therefore that your faith may be strengthened.' Thereupon he showed her the plates. My father and mother had a large family of their own, the addition to it therefore of Joseph, his wife Emma and Oliver very greatly increased the toil and anxiety of my mother. And although she had never complained she had sometimes felt that her labor was too much, or at least she was perhaps beginning to feel so. This circumstance, however, completely removed all such feelings and nerved her up for her increased responsibilities.

"Elder O. P.—Have you any idea when the other records will be brought forth?

"D. W.—When we see things in the spirit and by the power of God they seem to be right here; the present signs of the times indicate the near approach of the coming forth of the other plates, but when it will be I cannot tell. The three Nephites are at work among the lost tribes and elsewhere. John the Revelator is at work, and I believe the time will come suddenly, before we are prepared for it.

"Elder O. P.—Have you in your possession the original manuscripts of the Book of Mormon?

"D. W.—I have; they are in O. Cowdery's handwriting. He placed them in my care at his death, and charged me to preserve them as long as I lived; they are safe and well preserved.

"J. F. S.—What will be done with them at your death?

"D. W.—I will leave them to my

nephew, David Whitmer, son of my brother Jacob, and my namesake.

"O. P.—Would you not part with them to a purchaser?

"D. W.—No. Oliver charged me to keep them, and Joseph said my father's house should keep the records. I consider these things sacred, and would not part with nor barter them for money.

"J. F. S.—We would not offer you money in the light of bartering for the Mss., but we would like to see them preserved in some manner where they would be safe from casualties and from the caprices of men, in some institution that will not die as man does.

"D. W.—That is all right. While camping around here in a tent, all my effects exposed to the weather, everything in the trunk where the Mss were kept became mouldy, etc., but they were preserved, not even being discolored (we supposed his camping in a tent, etc., had reference to his circumstances after the cyclone, in June last), except only, as he and others affirm, the room in which the Mss. were kept. That was the only part of the house which was not demolished, and even the ceiling of that room was but little impaired. 'Do you think,' said Philander Page, a son of Hiram Page, one of the eight witnesses, 'that the Almighty cannot take care of His own?'"

We will next give the testimony of Oliver Cowdery. It is as given by him at a special conference held at Council Bluffs, on October 21st, 1848, his words being reported by the late Bishop Reuben Miller, of Mill Creek. He said:

"Friends and Brethren, my name is Cowdery—Oliver Cowdery. In the early history of this Church I stood identified with her, and one in her councils. True it is that the gifts and callings of God are without repentance. Not because I was better than the rest of mankind was I called; but, to fulfill the purposes of God, He called me to a high and holy calling. I wrote, with my own pen, the entire Book of Mormon (save a few pages), as it fell from the lips of the Prophet Joseph Smith, as he translated it by the gift and power of God, by

the means of the Urim and Thummim, or, as it is called by that book, 'holy interpreters.' *I beheld with my eyes and handled with my hands the gold plates from which it was translated.* I also saw with my eyes and handled with my hands the 'holy interpreters.' That book is *true*. Sidney Rigdon did not write it. Mr. Spaulding did not write it. I wrote it myself as it fell from the lips of the Prophet. It contains the everlasting gospel, and came forth to the children of men in fulfilment of the revelation of John, where he says he saw an angel come with the everlasting Gospel to preach to every nation, and kindred and people. It contains principles of salvation; and if you, my hearers, will walk by its light and obey its precepts, you will be saved with an everlasting salvation in the kingdom of God on high. Brother Hyde has just said that it is very important that we keep and walk in the true channel, in order to avoid sand-bars. This is true. The channel is here. The holy Priesthood is here. I was present with Joseph when an holy angel from God came down from heaven and conferred on us or restored the lesser or Aaronic Priesthood, and said to us, at the same time, that it should remain upon the earth while the earth stands. I was also present with Joseph when the higher or Melchisedek Priesthood was conferred by the holy angel from on high. This Priesthood was then conferred on each other, by the will and commandment of God. This Priesthood, as was then declared, is also to remain upon the earth until the last remnant of time. This holy Priesthood or authority we then conferred upon many, and is just as good and valid as though God had done it in person. I laid my hands upon that man—yes, I laid my right hand upon his head (pointing to Brother Hyde), and I conferred upon him this Priesthood, and he holds that Priesthood now. He was also called through me, by the prayer of faith, an Apostle of the Lord Jesus Christ."

And last comes the testimony of Martin Harris. From the various letters and other matter published by or regarding him, we extract the following, which is a portion of an interview between him and Elder D. B. Dille.

In answer to the inquiry, "What do you think of the Book of Mormon? Is it a divine record?" he answered: 'I was the right hand man of Joseph Smith, and I know that he was a prophet of God. I know the Book of Mormon is true—and you know that I know that it is true. I know that the plates have been translated by the gift and power of God, for His voice declared it unto us; therefore I know of a surety that the work is true; for did I not at one time hold the plates on my knee an hour and a half, while in conversation with Joseph, when we went to bury them in the woods, that the enemy might not obtain them? Yes I did. And as many of the plates as Joseph Smith translated, I handled with my hands, plate after plate.' Then, describing their dimensions, he pointed with one of the fingers of his left hand to the back of his right hand and said: 'I should think they were so long,' or about eight inches, 'and about so thick,' or about four inches; 'and each of the plates was thicker than the thickest of tin.'

"I then asked Mr. Harris if he ever lost three thousand dollars by the publishing of the Book of Mormon?

"Mr. Harris said, 'I never lost one cent. Mr. Smith paid me all that I advanced, and more too.' As much as to say he received a portion of the profits accruing from the sale of the books.

"Mr. Harris further said: 'I took a transcript of the characters of the plates to Dr. Anthon, of New York. When I arrived at the house of Professor Anthon, I found him in his office and alone, and presented the transcript to him, and asked him to read it. He said if I would bring the plates, he would assist in the translation. I told him I could not, for they were sealed. Professor Anthon then gave me a certificate certifying that the characters were Arabic, Chaldaic and Egyptian. I then left Dr. Anthon, and was near the door, when he said, 'How did the young man know the plates were there?' I said an angel had shown them to him. Professor Anthon then said, 'Let me see the certificate!' Upon which, I took it from my waistcoat pocket and unsuspectingly gave it to him. He then tore it up in anger, saying, there was no such things as angels now, it was all a hoax. I then went to Dr. Mitchell with the transcript, and he confirmed what Professor Anthon had said."

There is one point we wish to emphasize for the consideration of those who do not believe in the divinity of the Book of Mormon. It is the exact agreement of the statements of the three witnesses, (not only in the main points, but also in the minor details,) with regard to all the circumstances in which they were engaged connected with the coming forth and translation of that book. If any fraud had been practiced, or there had been a conspiracy to deceive the world, these witnesses in the lapse of so many years would doubtless have told conflicting and contradictory stories, especially in regard to minor points, but as it is, their statements are harmonious one with another, each building up and strengthening that which the others testify. Their testimony is unchangeable and undeviating, and the whole consistent with the narrative of the Prophet Joseph and the condition of things by which they were at that time surrounded.

TESTIMONY OF THE EIGHT WITNESSES.

The information contained in the "History of Joseph Smith" regarding the testimony of the eight witnesses is surprisingly meagre. It consists of but one single line, and is in these words: "Soon after these things had transpired, this additional testimony was obtained." Then follows the testimony as printed. The "these things" mentioned are the circumstances attending the reception of the angelic visitation by the three witnesses. So all we know is that shortly after the testimony of the three witnesses was received, Joseph obtained the testimony of the eight; but we are not informed whether he showed the plates to all the eight at once, or at various times, or whether some of them had seen the plates at times anterior to the day they were seen by the three. These items, of course, are of minor importance while the central truth remains intact that they handled, lifted and examined the plates. These eight, like the three, never denied their testimony. All are now dead, and all, except one, died faithful in the Church. That one was John Whitmer; and even he, though he had turned from the truth, yet, in the midst of mobocratic violence, still adhered to his testimony when that testimony was liable to bring trouble upon his head, as the following extract from the "History of Joseph Smith," under date of April 5th, 1839, shows. The circumstance there related occurred at the time Joseph and others of the brethren were confined in prison at Liberty, Missouri, and the conversation took place in the presence of a number of mobocrats.

[Theodore] "Turley said: 'Gentlemen, I presume there are men here who have heard Corrill say 'Mormonism' was true, Joseph Smith was a Prophet and inspired of God, etc. I now call upon you, John Whitmer: You say Corrill* is a moral and good man; do you believe him, when he says the Book of Mormon is true, or when it is not true?' There are many things published that they say are true, and again turn round and say it is false.' Whitmer asked, 'Do you hint at me?' Turley replied, 'If the cap fits you, wear it; all I know, you have published to the world that an angel did present those plates to Joseph Smith. Whitmer replied, 'I now say, I handled those plates; there were fine engravings on both sides. I handled them;' and he described how they were hung, and 'they were shown to me by a supernatural power;' he acknowledged all. Turley asked him, 'Why the translation is not now here?' He said, 'I cannot read it, and I do not know whether it is true or not.' Whitmer testified all this in the presence of eight men."

Incidental to the publication of the first edition of the Book of Mormon, the Prophet says in his history:

"I wish to mention here, that the title

* John Corrill, who apostatized in Missouri and wrote a work on "Mormonism."

page of the Book of Mormon is a literal translation, taken from the very last leaf on the left hand side of the collection or book of plates which contained the record which has been translated, the language of the whole running the same as all Hebrew writing in general; and that said title page is not by any means a modern composition either of mine or any other man's who has lived or does live in this generation. Therefore, in order to correct an error which generally exists concerning it, I give below that part of the title page of the English version of the Book of Mormon, which is a genuine and literal translation of the title page of the original Book of Mormon, as recorded on the plates:

"The Book of Mormon, an account written by the hand of Mormon, upon plates, taken from the plates of Nephi.

"Wherefore it is an abridgment of the record of the people of Nephi, and also of the Lamanites; written to the Lamanites, who are a remnant of the house of Israel; and also to Jew and Gentile; written by way of commandment, and also by the spirit of prophecy and revelation.

"Written and sealed up, and hid up unto the Lord, that they might not be destroyed—to come forth by the gift and power of God unto the interpretation thereof—sealed by the hand of Moroni, and hid up unto the Lord, to come forth in due time by the way of Gentile—the interpretation thereof by the gift of God.

"An abridgment taken from the book of Ether, also, which is a record of the people of Jared, who were scattered at the time the Lord confounded the language of the people when they were building a tower to get to heaven; which is to shew unto the remnant of the house of Israel what great things the Lord hath done for their fathers; and that they may know the covenants of the Lord, that they are not cast off for ever; and also to the convincing of the Jew and Gentile that Jesus is the Christ, the eternal God, manifesting himself unto all nations. And now, if there are faults, they are the mistakes of men; wherefore condemn not the things of God, that ye may be found spotless at the judgment seat of Christ.

"The remainder of the title page is, of course, modern."

As might reasonably be expected, considering the peculiar circumstances under which it was printed, some few, though mostly unimportant typographical errors, crept into this first edition. These were mostly corrected in the third edition, the revision being made, as we have been informed, under the personal supervision of the Prophet Joseph Smith. During the time that President George A. Smith was Church Historian, a careful and exhaustive comparison of the two editions was made in his office, and it was found that the corrections only amounted to about thirty in number; and these were generally verbal or grammatical alterations. For instance the following changes were found to have been made:

*67 my to they,
83 hath to had,

380 went to sent,
387 prisoners to provisions,
453 sign to signal,
521 Angelah to Angola.

In some few cases the difference is somewhat greater, as:

38 preparation to foundation,
31 That state of awful woundedness to awful state of blindness.

In seven instances omissions of words or parts of sentences have been supplied; and in fifteen, corrections have been made by omitting superfluous words or tautological expressions.

George Reynolds.

* The figures refer to the pages in the first edition.

THE CHILDREN.

When the lessons and tasks are all ended,
  And the school for the day is dismissed,
The little ones gather around me,
  To bid me good-night, and be kissed;
Oh, the little white arms that encircle
  My neck in their tender embrace!
Oh, the smiles that are halos of heaven,
  Shedding sunshine of love on my face!

And when they are gone I sit dreaming
  Of my childhood too lovely to last;
Of joy that my heart will remember,
  While it wakes to the pulse of the past,
Ere the world and its wickedness made me
  A partner of sorrow and sin,
When the glory of God was about me,
  And the glory of gladness within.

All my heart grows as weak as a woman's,
  And the fountains of feeling will flow,
When I think of the paths steep and stony,
  Where the feet of the dear ones must go,—
Of the mountains of sin hanging o'er them,
  Of the tempests of Fate blowing wild;
Ah, there's nothing on earth half so holy
  As the innocent heart of a child!

They are idols of hearts and of households;
  They are angels of God in disguise;
His sunlight still sleeps in their tresses,
  His glory still gleams in their eyes;
Those truants from home and from heaven—
  They have made me more manly and mild;
And I know now how Jesus could liken
  The Kingdom of God to a child!

I ask not a life for the dear ones,
  All radiant, as others have done,
But that life may have just enough shadow
  To temper the glare of the sun;
I would pray God to guard them from evil,
  But my prayer would bound back to myself;
Ah! a seraph may pray for a sinner,
  But a sinner must pray for himself.

The twig is so easily bended,
  I have banished the rule and the rod;
I have taught them the goodness of knowledge,
  They have taught me the goodness of God.
My heart is the dungeon of darkness,
  Where I shut them for breaking a rule;
My frown is sufficient correction;
  My love is the law of the school.

I shall leave the old house in the Autumn,
  To traverse its threshold no more;
Ah! how I shall sigh for the dear ones,
  That meet me each morn at the door!
I shall miss the "good-nights" and the kisses,
  And the gush of their innocent glee,
The group on the green, and the flowers
  That are brought every morning for me.

I shall miss them at morn and at even,
  Their song in the school and the street;
I shall miss the low hum of their voices,
  And the tread of their delicate feet.
When the lessons of life are all ended,
  And death says, "The school is dismissed!"
May the little ones gather around me,
  To bid me good-night and be kissed.

Charles M. Dickinson.

POLITICAL INSTITUTIONS.

v.

THE extent and limit of governmental powers relative to the commercial interests of society vary greatly among the different civilized nations of the earth. The functions of government in the regulations of trade are, too, taking a distinctive range in the direction of existing political discussions of our own country. Ever since this nation assumed control of its own commerce, Congress has deemed it to be its duty to protect the interests of the people by modifying the natural intercourse of international products. A political superstition or tradition, that the more the government has to do with the business interests of the people at large, the greater the prosperity. A fact patent to every student of history, that there has been a gradual decline in the power which nations have possessed to control the lands and work out the channels of trade, is not wanting. Among the Romans the land was the property of the state. The state was more a natural person in its powers than an artificial one, and whatever rights individuals acquired, they considered them a beneficent endowment of the parent government.

The theory that the government could create rights has gradually broken down until the most advanced nations have begun to consider its government an artificial personage, holding only those powers which its constituents confer upon it. England has step by step given up the ownership of her soil and allowed her citizens to become landholders; but the great difficulties of the present system of landholding in England are directly or indirectly traceable to governmental interference. The absence, therefore, of State meddling with lands and commerce generally is characteristic of national and material progress.

The United States believed that to increase the prosperity of its people and establish home industry, it became necessary to regulate the natural intercourse between us and other nations,

hence a protective tariff. And as great landlords grew up in England by her interference with the lands, so great monopolies have grown up in this country under the tariff system. But the protectionist (aggressionist) will say it at once opened home manufactures and started these industries long before they could otherwise have been commenced. What would the people of Utah say if a tax indirectly were levied upon them to start silk factories. What would be the result? Capital which should be used for the development of the soil and most available resources of the country would be withdrawn and put into silk factories. The people of a new country naturally find stock raising most profitable at first, then comes farming and afterwards manufactures, and any artificial means employed to reverse so natural an order must prove detrimental to the community at large. It would be just as consistent for the people of a Territory to claim a protective tariff in order to give capitalists an opportunity to make silk and woolen goods, as it is for the general government to discriminate against the whole people as consumers in favor of a few as manufacturers. Protectionists try to evade the comparison by saying that we are one politically, and therefore should be one commercially, while at the same time they must acknowledge that the new divisions of our country bear the same relative position commercially that America does with England.

New countries have natural advantages over old ones and *vice versa*, why not let these differences suffice, and make no discriminations, for discriminations always produce an unnatural class distinction hurtful to the interests of the majority. The wail goes up that we cannot compete with the pauper and prison labor of the old world. Let us stop for a moment and examine this pet theory of the protectionist, prick the bubble and see how much solid argument it contains. In the first place the great majority of the workingmen in the old world are not prisoners or paupers; how can they compete with pauper and prison labor. They make no great disturbance over it, and it is seldom or never mentioned among them. We make a wonderful bluster about it way off here, while those at home who would be the first, naturally, to complain of such labor never exhibit the least concern. If there were anything about it but shallow sophistry, the regular workmen of the old world would raise as great a howl over prison and pauper labor as we do over the Chinese question.

In the next place these prisoners wont and cannot be made to work with the same interest that regular workmen have. Recently while visiting Blackwell's Island, I remarked to the superintendent that the city must profit considerably from convict labor of the hundreds there confined. With a look of absurdity he remonstrated by saying that it required about all their labor was worth to get the little out of them that they did. We have convict labor in our own country, but it never occurs to the laborer or the aggressionist that we should lament their competition; but the tariff man will manufacture a pitiful story, and draw the gloomiest picture of prison labor thousands of miles away. Anciently the crafty sought religious ghosts to frighten the people into wretched submission, now it is a political ghost in the form of prison labor.

A correspondent of the Philadelphia *Times*, who had gone to England, some time ago, to establish a particular branch of American industry wrote that journal to the effect that the English laborer was about as well off as the American, and he saw and heard comparatively nothing of prison and pauper labor, so much talked about in the United States. In a recent discussion over tariff with a gentleman I met on the train, he compared the condition of the people of British America, where free trade prevails, with that of the United States under protection. I remonstrated by saying that the difference was due rather to the industrial habits and inge-

nuity of the people of the two countries than to any artificial difference which governments could create. If tariff makes the difference between the prosperity of the people of the United States and British America, what makes the difference between England and British America, or England and the East Indies, or the Australians, or go still farther between the English and the Hotentots? It is nonsense to talk about tariff making the differences which exist in the prosperity of different peoples. The differences are to be sought for in their physical and mental constitutions.

I was a short time ago in the southern part of Canada and took the trouble to inquire into the habits and life of the Canadians. They were not reported as an industrious people. Along the rivers and lakes they were fishers and hunters, and in Michigan considered the lowest class. The aggressionists in Utah hold up our lead traffic and say what would become of Utah if the tariff were taken off from lead. It reminds me of the freight agitation which our freighters raised on the advent of railroads. Most of our readers will remember the almost universal prophetic declarations that the railroads would kill Utah, for freighting was the chief source of our money. Teams would be worthless, they said, and money would all be taken out of the country. What were the facts? New channels for new and extended industries opened and prosperity increased. No man was able to point out the new channels, but the industry of the people and their ingenuity established them. Do those who talk of our lead industries mean to say that even their total extinction will kill the industry and ambition of the people? Give the people more for their money and they will need less money.

On the train from Chicago to East Saginaw, I fell in the company of one of the delegates of the latter place to the Democratic National Convention. He was a member of the committee who drew up the platform; and when I asked him why the party was neither protectionists nor free traders, but stood, straddle of the fence, he explained by saying that there was an immense amount of capital invested on the strength of a heavy tariff, and that it would not do to let the flood gates of free trade open upon them and sink their money. He thought they should be let down gradually. He evidently did not discriminate between the functions of party principles and the law-making body. Why should the party compromise? The conservative ones should be the law makers, not the party. Congress must work to the principles as they are destined to lead to the final result, and that final result should be declared by the party that its constituents may know what is actually meant.

I do not believe in protection even for revenue only. In the first place if the States were taxed, the people would feel and realize more keenly the burden of such a direct tax. They would look after their law makers and see that they did not squander so much money. They would reverse the dangerous political order of regarding our congressmen and legislators generally. Instead of thinking matters were going right until it was proven that they were going wrong, they would begin to think that they were going wrong until it was proven that they were going right. Finally, if taxation were direct, the burden of government would fall more upon the shoulders of the rich who own the property, and less upon the poor. Whereas indirect taxation falls more upon the poor, who are the majority of the consumers. Well but wouldn't wages fall if free trade were established? Certainly, but the cost of living would be correspondingly less, so that if the working man pays less for the necessaries of life, he can afford to work for less. *J. M. Tanner.*

When there is much pretension, much has been borrowed; nature never pretends.—*Lavater.*

REMARKABLE DREAMS.

THE present times seem to be more than usually prolific of prophetic dreams among the Latter-day Saints. In nearly every settlement the people have been warned of events soon to occur; and visions of the future glory of the Kingdom of God upon this earth have passed like a panorama before many of those who love God and obey His commandments.

Some two or three years ago, I had retired for the night, when suddenly a glorious messenger appeared at my bedside and awoke me from my slumber. The light of his presence filled the room, so that objects were discerned as clearly as at noonday.

He handed me a book, saying, "Look, and see what is coming to pass." I took the book in my hands and, sitting up in bed, examined it carefully and read its contents. In size this book was about seven by ten inches, opening like a copy-book and bound in beautiful covers, on the front of which was stamped in gold letters its title, which was THE BOOK OF THE PLAGUES. The leaves were printed only on the front side of each, and were composed of the very finest quality of pure white linen, instead of paper. The typography throughout was in the finest style of the printer's art. Each page was composed of a picture printed in colors as natural as art can copy nature, which occupied the upper half of the space, below which was the printed description of the scene represented.

On the first page was a picture of a feast in progress, with the long table set upon a beautiful lawn, over which were interspersed clumps of fine shrubs and towering trees. In the background through the foliage, could be discerned a stately suburban villa, adorned with all the ornaments of modern architecture. The landscape presented the appearance of midsummer. The sky, and indeed the whole atmosphere, appeared of a peculiar sickly brassy hue, similar to that which may be observed when the sun is wholly eclipsed, and the disc is just beginning again to give its light. Throughout the atmosphere small white specks were represented, similar to a scattering fall of minute snow flakes in winter. About the table a party of richly dressed ladies and gentlemen were seated in the act of partaking of the rich repast with which the table was laden. The minute specks falling from above were dropping into the food apparently unheeded by all, for a sudden destruction had come upon them. Many were falling backward in the agonies of a fearful death; others drooping upon the table, and others pausing with their hands still holding the untasted food, their countenances betraying a fearful astonishment at the peculiar and unlooked for condition of their companions. Death was in the atmosphere; the judgments of God had come upon them as silently and swiftly as upon the proud Sennacharib and his host of Assyrians.

In one corner of this picture was a small circular vignette, showing the front of the store of a dealer in pork. The wide sidewalk was covered by an awning supported on posts at the outer edge, and on this walk were shown barrels of pork, long strings of sausages, fresh slaughtered hogs, piles of smoked bacon and headcheese; and along the edge of the walk, next to the store, beneath the front windows, leaned a number of large hams and pieces of side meat, reaching across the whole front, except a small space at the doorway. There were twelve of these pieces, and on each piece was painted a large letter, in order to make as a whole the word ABOMINATIONS.

Below this scene was the description: *A Feast among the Gentiles, commencement of the Plague.* And in smaller type below, a note saying that the particles of poison, though represented in the picture, are so small as to be invisible to the naked eye.

On the next page was another picture. It was a street scene in a large city. In the foreground were the residences of wealthy city merchants. The character of the buildings gradually changed; along the view and in the distance were shown the great buildings of trade and commerce in the heart of a large metropolis. On the sidewalks throughout the long vista, the busy, throbbing, rushing crowd had been cut down like grass before the mower.

Again it was a midsummer scene. The same atoms of poison were falling through the air, but their work was done; the same sickly brazen atmosphere that seemed thick with foul odors laid upon the earth, in which no breeze stirred a leaf of the foliage. Upon the balconies of the richly decorated residences, across the thresholds of the opened doorways, along the walks and upon the crossings, lay the men, women and children, who a few days before were enjoying all the pleasures of life. Further on, the dead were everywhere. Houses of business that had been thronged with customers stood with open doorways, frowning upon streets covered with the dead. Across the thresholds of the banks lay the guardians of wealth, but no thieves were there to take the unlocked treasures within. The costly merchandise of a thousand owners laid untouched upon the counters and shelves. In the noonday glare of the sickly sun, not a soul was shown alive; not one had been left to bury the dead—all had been stricken or had fled from the death-dealing plague and the doomed city. Along midway upon the street, a hungry drove of those horrible ugly slaughterhouse hogs, (which may be seen in the pens attached to the filthy slaughtering places in the outskirts of many cities), was tearing and devouring the dead and feasting upon the bodies of rich and poor alike with none to molest them.

Below this picture was the description: *Progress of the Plague among the Gentiles. A street scene in a large city.* Nearly fifty of these pictures I carefully observed, wherein the fearful effects of this and other plagues were almost as vividly portrayed as if I had actually seen them.

The last scene in the book was descriptive of the same plague as the first. A beautiful park-like, grassy prairie was surrounded by elm and cottonwood trees, the area embraced being about eighty rods across. In the centre of this enclosure was a large cone-shaped tent of a bright purple color, about thirty feet in height by twenty in diameter at the base. Midway in height in this tent was a floor dividing the inside into two stories. Near this tent was another, a round wall tent, about thirty feet in diameter, and nearly as high as the first. This was clean and white. Leaving a space of about a hundred yards from these central tents were hundreds of small rectangular wall tents in rows, reaching as far as the surrounding trees, each tent clean and white, and appearing to be of a size suited to the wants of an ordinary family. Not a human being, animal, bird or vehicle was in sight. Not a breath of air appeared to be stirring. The same atmosphere as in the previous pictures, with the atoms of poison, was represented, and the same time and season of the year.

Below this picture was the description: "A camp of the Saints who have gathered together and are living under the daily revelations of God, and are thus preserved from the plague." I understood from this that each family was in its tent during the hours of the day that the poison falls, and thus were preserved from breathing the deathly particles.

Handing the book to the messenger, who all this time had remained by my side, he vanished from my view as suddenly as he had appeared. I awoke my wife, who was soundly sleeping, and commenced to relate to her what I had just beheld. After telling her the description of the two pictures at the beginning of the book, and commencing on the third, this third picture and all up to the last was suddenly taken from my memory, so that I have never been able to recall them; but still I remember that they were scenes about the plagues and judgments.

In the revelations given to the Prophet Joseph, among the many plagues and judgments portrayed, that given in the Doctrine and Covenants, Sec. xxix: 17—20, has always seemed to me to fully coincide with what has been related in the account of that dream. But whether that plague or another is meant, it does not matter. Plagues will come and the wicked must suffer; but the Saints will be preserved by the very principle for which the wicked persecute them, which is present revelation from the Almighty. *Add-Caput-Ville.*

The curious traveling stones of Australia are paralleled in Nevada. They are described as almost perfectly round, about as large as a walnut, and of an ivory nature. When distributed about upon a level surface, within two or three feet of each other, they will begin traveling toward a common center, and there lie huddled up in a bunch, like a lot of eggs in a nest. A single stone, removed to a distance of three and a half feet, upon being released, returns to the heap, but at four or five feet lies motionless. They are composed of magnetic iron ore.

THE QUEEN'S HOUSEHOLD.

NOMINALLY the principal officer of the Queen's household is the Lord Chamberlain, who is a peer of the realm, draws two thousand pounds a year, and plays a large part at coronations, royal marriages, christenings and funerals. Actually, up to within a recent date, the principal personage in the household of Queen Victoria was a Scotch gillie, who brought to London his kilt and his bare legs, which always formed a prominent feature in any public appearance of the Queen. There is not known, at least in modern history, a parallel to the precise position which John Brown held in the Queen's household. His title was "Personal Attendant," and he literally fulfilled it, going out with Her Majesty on whatever errand she might appear, whether driving in state to open a session of Parliament, hurrying in a pony-carriage under the wet skies of Balmoral, or walking or riding amid the beauties of the Italian lakes.

The Queen has herself recorded, in simple language, the early growth of the attachment to the Scotch gillie. None but he could lead her pony over the Scotch mountain passes, and when the then young Queen had to be carried some distance, it was John Brown who, perhaps having read something of Sir Walter Raleigh, took off his plaid, and wrapping the Queen in it, he and another bore her bundle-wise over the pass. The last time John Brown appeared in public pageantry was at the opening of the Law Courts in the Strand. There was a magnificent procession of all that was great and famous in England. Peers and Commons, with Mr. Gladstone at their head in the stately robes of Chancellor of the Exchequer; judges in their scarlet and ermine, looking as if they had stepped out of a burlesque; Col. Fred Burnaby, "Silver-Stick-in-Waiting," — a most massive "Stick," six feet four in length, and burly to boot, looking bigger than ever in his tight white leather trousers, his gigantic boots and his short jacket; Bishops, Archbishops, Prince of Wales the Princess of Wales and the rest of the Royal family; and then a stout, well made man in Highland costume, who walked with head erect amongst the best of them, serene in the unmeasured confidence of his sovereign. This was John Brown; and when the procession halted, and the Queen of England, surrounded by her nobles, stood and faced the scarcely less brilliant throng that filled the hall, there were doubtless as many eyes turned upon plain John Brown as upon the Archbishop of York, or the Home Secretary. A few months later John Brown was dead, and through the official Court Circular the Queen proclaimed her sorrow in words singularly similar to those in which, a year or two

back, she had lamented the death of her trusty counselor, the Earl of Beaconsfield.

In all there are in the Queen's household just under a thousand persons, each with his appointed post and sufficient salary, for the maintenance of whom the nation sets apart the sum of three hundred and eighty-five thousand pounds. The Lord Chamberlain is assisted by a Vice-Chamberlain, who draws a salary of nine hundred and twenty-four pounds. This, like the Lord Chamberlainship, is a political office, and is held by a member of the House of Commons. The Keeper of Her Majesty's Privy Purse has two thousand pounds a year, which, considering that the privy purse is not filled with more than sixty thousand pounds, is not an illiberal recompense. The office is not a laborious one, all Her Majesty's needs being provided for under other heads in the grants for the various departments of the household. This sixty thousand pounds a year is understood to be transferred pretty much in a lump sum to those "savings" for which Queen Victoria rightly or wrongly receives credit from the popular mind.

In this same department ranks the Mistress of the Robes, who receives five hundred pounds a year; a Groom of the Robes, who has eight hundred pounds, and Ladies of the Bedchamber, of whom there are eight, at a salary of five hundred pounds a year each. These ladies rarely rank under a duchess, and always belong to the highest families. It will be remembered that the Queen was barely seated on the throne, when the Constitution was shaken by what was known as the bedchamber question. Sir Robert Peel, being in a position of great difficulty, required the removal of certain ladies who were closely allied with his political opponents. The Queen stood by her rights, declared she would not be dictated to in the matter of her bedchamber. Sir Robert Peel assented to the principle, but at the same time resigned, and was not to be brought back till he gained his way. An arrangement is made by which the Ladies of the Bedchamber are in attendance for a fortnight at a time. They settle the turns among themselves, and usually get three a year. The Maids of Honor, of whom there are likewise eight, receive a salary of three hundred pounds a year each, and are in attendance in couples for a month at a time.

Formerly both Maids of Honor and Bedchamber Women were under strict discipline, and really did some work for their wages. The Countess of Suffolk, in her correspondence, lifts the veil and allows us to peep at majesty served by its Bedchamber Women. "The Bedchamber Women came into waiting before the Queen's prayers," writes the Duchess, "which was before she was dressed. * * When the Queen washed her hands, the Page of the Back-Stairs brought and set down on the side table the basin and ewer. Then the Bedchamber Woman set it before the Queen and knelt on the other side of the table, over against the Queen, the Bedchamber Lady only looking on. The Bedchamber Woman poured the water out of the ewer upon the Queen's hand. The Bedchamber Woman pulled on the Queen's gloves when she could not do it herself. The Page of the Back-Stairs was called in to put on the Queen's shoes. When the Queen dined in public, the Page reached the glass to the Bedchamber Woman and she to the Lady in Waiting. The Bedchamber Woman brought the chocolate and gave it without kneeling."

Services of this kind are not confined to women. There are Lords in Waiting, who do about as much as Ladies in Waiting. These receive the oddly precise sum of seven hundred and two pounds a year. Of lower rank are the Grooms in Waiting, who receive £335.12.6 per annum apiece. There are four Gentleman Ushers of the Privy Chamber, at two hundred pounds per annum; four Daily Waiters, at one hundred and fifty pounds, and four Grooms of the Privy Chamber, at the modest recompense of seventy-three pounds per annum. But though the income is small, these offices are eagerly competed for, and are held by Vice-Admirals, Colonels and other distinguished personages.

There are five Pages of the Back-Stairs—not a lofty description, but the salary is fair, reaching four hundred pounds per annum. These gentlemen really have work to do. They wait at the royal dinner table, and one is always in attendance at the door of Her Majesty's apartment from eight in the morning until she retires for the night. There are six pages of the Presence, so called, apparently, because they do not actually dwell in the Presence, their duties being to attend upon the Lords, Ladies and Maids of Honor, and upon any of Her Majesty's visitors. For this they receive one hundred and eighty pounds a year; There are nine Housekeepers and upwards of sixty Housemaids. The Household has its ecclesiastical staff. The Bishop of London is always Dean of the Chapel Royal, and draws for his service a salary of two hundred pounds a year. There is a complete sanitary establishment at a cost to the tax-payers of two thousand seven hundred pounds a year. This consists of two Physicians in Ordinary, four Physicians Extraordinary, four Apothecaries for the Queen herself, and two for the combined Household, one Dentist, an Aurist, an Oculist and a Surgeon-Chiropodist. There is also a Poet Laureate, at the present time Lord Tennyson, who receives one hundred pounds a year, a sum that seems insignificant beside the income of one of the Pages of the Back-Stairs. The sister-art of painting is even more shabbily treated, the Painter in Ordinary receiving only fifty pounds a year.

More clearly pertaining to the Household, in the ordinary acceptation of the word, is the department of the Lord Steward. Like the Lord Chamberlain, he is a Peer of the Realm, a friend of the government of the day, and the recipient of two thousand pounds a year. His functions are defined in the same precision as those of the Lord Chancellor or the Commander-in-Chief. It is written that "the estate of the Queen's Household is entirely committed to the Lord Steward to be ruled and governed according to his discretion. All his rules and commands in court are to be obeyed." His authority reaches over all the Officers and Servants of the Queen's Household, excepting those of the Queen's Chamber, Stable and Chapel. He has authority to hold courts for administering justice and settling disputes among the domestic servants of the Queen. He is assisted by a Treasurer and Controller of the Household, who each receives nine hundred and four pounds per annum. The Master of the Household has one thousand one hundred and fifty-eight pounds a year and practically does the work of the Lord Steward.

There is a Clerk of the Kitchen, whose importance is indicated by his salary of seven hundred pounds a year. The Chief Cook draws the same sum. There are four Master Cooks, who have a salary of six pounds a week, with the privilege of taking four apprentices, whom they charge premiums of from one hundred and fifty pounds to two hundred pounds. There are two Yeomen of the Kitchen, two assistant Cooks, two Roasting Cooks, four Scourers, three Kitchen-Maids, a Store-Keeper and two Steam-Apparatus Men—this last a modern addition to the Royal Household unknown at the time of Henry VIII, who was a family man, and paid much attention to the regulation of the Household, and established precedents many of which exist to this day. There is a Gentleman of Wine and Beer Cellars, who draws five hundred pounds a year, and has the duty of purchasing wines for the Royal establishment. He has under him two Yeomen at one hundred and fifty pounds a year, and a Groom at eighty pounds. There is a Principal Table-Decker, who has two hundred pounds a year, is assisted by a second Table-Decker at one hundred and fifty pounds, a third at ninety pounds, and an assistant at fifty-two pounds. There is also a Wax-fitter, who sees the candles properly disposed, whilst the Deckers lay the dinner-cloth, and see that the plates, dishes and cutlery are fairly set forth.

Furthermore, there is quite an army of porters, at the head of whom is the First Gentleman Porter; but as may be supposed, it would be a mistake to ask him to take your portmanteau upstairs upon arrival at one of the royal palaces. He probably looks around and sees that the First and Second Yeomen Porters, the Assistant Porter and the three Groom Porters do their work. There are a First and Second Lamplighter at one hundred pounds each a year, nearly twice as much as is paid to the Wax-fitter, and just the same as the Poet Laureate is thought to be worth. There is also a Barge-master and Waterman, who get four hundred pounds a year, although there is now no royal barge, nor any going to and fro by water, as was once the wont of English Majesty.

This list does not comprise the full muster of the Queen's household, but it may sufficiently indicate its vastness and its dignity. There is one personage who should not be omitted from the list, and though he comes last, he is by no means least. This is the Queen's Rat-Catcher, who is specially attached to Buckingham Palace. A peculiarity about this personage is that he is provided for outside the civil list. His salary is fifteen pounds a year, and every session the House of Commons, being on Committee of Supply, considers this vote, and gravely agrees to it. It is not much, little more than a hundredth part of the salary of the Hereditary Grand Falconer, who has twelve hundred pounds a year. But these are persons who draw their money from the treasury of the Royal household, and to that extent rank as servants. The Rat-Catcher is of the household, and yet apart from it. He resides near the scene of his labors, and his fifteen pounds a year, proposed by a Minister of the Crown, is voted with all the machinery of Parliament going at high pressure.—*Youth's Companion.*

No one is so blind to his own faults as a man who has the habit of detecting the faults of others.

Relieve misfortune quickly. A man is like an egg—the longer he is kept in hot water, the harder he is when taken out.

THE ARMY.

I.

PHILOSOPHERS have derived much satisfaction from a circumstance growing out of the late rebellion. Great Britain was disposed, for various historical and commercial reasons, to cast its sympathies with the Southern States, and, as far as consistent with the rules of international law, to countenance their struggles for independence. To express sympathy for them, even to the extent of recognizing their independence, was proper; but not so the open and notorious use of a British harbor for the building and partial equipment of the "Alabama" and other less widely known rebel cruisers.

The rebellion ended, the Federal government endeavored to secure an adjustment of this breach of comity, and demanded reparation from England, for the great damage she had rendered possible to our merchant marine. A war seemed imminent; the analogies of history suggested it, and the passions of the citizens of both countries would have countenanced it. But, singularly enough, reason prevailed; the dispute was submitted to arbitration, and the horrors of war averted by the payment to the Unted States of fifteen million dollars. It was this anomalous proceeding, so full of promise for the future, that inspired the hopes of those who fancied they beheld the dawn of the day of reason, before the twilight of the day of war had faded.

But such hopes were premature; war is still waged. The life of the individual is but the diminutive of that of the nation. The latter has its birth, its period of infancy, youth, manhood, decrepitude, and, finally, its day of dissolution. Draper, in writing the "Intellectual Development of Europe," has traced the life of each of the nations of Europe through all or some of these stages. Not only may we trace a parallel between the physical development of the individual and that of the state, but in one we may find the same characteristics of mind

11*

and passion which are evinced by the other. As the individual is actuated by sentiments of love or hate, so is the nation; as the former is prompted by motives of jealousy or revenge, in a similar way do we find nations thus moved.

The individual has learned that it is wise to submit difficulties to courts for settlement; likewise have nations concluded that boards of arbitrators and international courts are beneficial institutions. Yet, individuals are by passion led into personal encounters; and similarly nations rise up in arms for the adjustment of those wrongs, which are inflicted with gross insult. In primitive society might was right; by strength property was acquired; by strength it was retained; there was no justice but force, no mercy but might; there were no courts but battlefields, and the victors were the judges.

The nation and the individual have plodded along through the dim past hand in hand, ever becoming less bloody and ferocious, and more regardful of the peace and happiness of society and the rights of fellows, until now we find war less frequent and atrocious, moderated by rules and the influences of religion.

In tracing the military development of the world, we find the same rate of improvement that has characterized other professions. In weapons, advance was early made from the club and sling to the spear and sword and shield. The Greeks and Romans used these weapons together with chariots, bows and arrows and others of a similar character, either their own invention or the heritage of other nations. They also protected their heads and bodies by armor. Cities were walled from a very early day. In the storming of fortified sites vast engines for propelling stones, battering rams, movable towers and Greek fire, were brought to a great degree of perfection at an early period. These and similar devices continued to be the instruments of attack and defence until the application of gunpowder to the art of war. Since which time there has been progression from the cumbrous flintlock of uncertain fire and aim to the deadly long range gun of the modern infantry. From the catapult it was a long step to the clumsy ordnance of the early days of gunpowder; but it has been a longer step from the culverin of the middle ages to the one hundred ton guns of the present day. Similarly the fortification of cities has been reduced to the most perfect science, and the armament of ships has been extended so far that now vessels of war are pointed out to us with walls of steel and wood several feet in thickness. The sling has been replaced by the Gatling guns and the Hotchkiss revolving cannon, which literally pour forth showers of lead. The torpedo, a submarine enemy, renders precarious the existence of the heaviest ironclad; other torpedoes, guided by electricity, move through the water, here and there, at pleasure. A gun which throws dynamite is the latest engine of destruction. The cannon is still being enlarged and improved in order that the sides of the ironclad may be penetrated; the sides of the ironclad are being thickened and strengthened in order that resistance may be effectually offered.

Strategy has remained unchanged. We find Napoleon fighting his battles on the same plans made use of by Cæsar and Hannibal. The objects of a commander are still to oppose a superior force to an inferior one, to turn the enemy's flanks, to penetrate his centre, to cut off his line of communications. Tactics have undergone such changes as were rendered necessary by the improvement of weapons.

With primitive weapons, deep masses of men, ranks behind ranks, were found most effectual. The Grecian phalanx and the Roman legion were masses of troops, which, by reason of mere mass and momentum were found irresistible. Cavalry, which in the middle ages became the principal arm, was at this early period, as now, a mere adjunct to the more important infantry arm. At the time of the crusades, during the age of chivalry, nearly all fighting was of a desultory character; large armies were comparatively unknown, and war was waged by bands of mounted knights and their retainers. Somewhat later the value of infantry was again demonstrated; this time by the Swiss, who were compelled to adopt the method of warfare on foot by the natural ruggedness of their native country. Several Swiss victories over the proud knights of Austria, had the effect of bringing mounted troops into disrepute. Since this time they have continued to grow of less importance, until now they are but a small proportion of an army, and are used not so much in the battle itself as for such duty as cutting lines of communication, for picket and raiding services, and, of course, in Indian warfare.

With a gun so imperfect as the old "blunderbuss," requiring thirty-two motions in the execution of the command "load," and of such inaccurate fire and short range, it would of course result that ranks would still be deep and that mass would be an important factor where hand to hand fighting was still possible. But as the gun was improved in range and effect it was found that the massing of men must be avoided; and so from the time of Gustavus Adolphus, who fought with six ranks, I believe, the number of ranks has continually decreased until now but two ranks are used in the drill and the movements of troops, while a single rank, at open intervals, supported by similar lines, is almost exclusively used in battle.

While the mere lighting of a battle or campaign is done with much more scientific weapons than were known to Cæsar or even to Napoleon, yet we find that the principle of strategy which either applied, stand to-day as the perfection of military generalship. Youths in military schools are taught the principles upon which the battle of Pharsalia was fought, they are thoroughly instructed in the many campaigns and encounters of Napoleon; while our late civil war is considered so barren of what is regarded as the highest in war, that its many campaigns are passed over in silence.

To say, however, that our war was not fought strategically, is not to say that it was not fought bravely, since in the one great battle at Gettysburg the casualties were more numerous than during the entire Franco-Prussian war. As a rule the number of killed and disabled in a modern battle with improved methods, is less, proportionately, than in the struggles of ancient days. Hand to hand encounters were prolific of casualties. It may be questioned, then, how a war accomplishes the end aimed at or feared. It is because of its vast expense under modern methods, and of the injury inflicted upon commerce; because of the accumulated wealth of the warring nations and the further losses probable to the unsuccessful combatants, which should prolong the conflict. France wars with Germany; the ground remains untilled, the looms unworked, her fleets are drawn from the seas, and the very arteries and veins of national existence are clogged. France has already expended hundreds of millions of francs, her people are out of employment; starvation fronts them; disgrace and further humiliation await her; she still has existence, she can better afford to indemnify the Germans than prolong the controversy.

The inhabitants of Europe are to-day groaning under the military loads they have to bear. They are heavily taxed to support millions of armed men and furnish the munitions of war; they are impressed into the service at the sacrifice of business hopes and social aspirations. And yet it would be folly for any one of these nations to disarm without a general disarmament. The latter has been discussed, but all are suspicious of their neighbors. It will be a long stride towards the millennial reign of peace, when the people of Europe are freed from the intolerable burdens of military despotism.

It is with feelings of satisfaction that we turn to the contemplation of the United States in this respect as in many others. We feel no military yoke, as we feel no yoke of kingly power or prerogative. While European nations are forced to arm themselves against the jealousies and ambition of their neighbors, we, by reason of isolation or the weakness of our neighbors, are freed from such burdens. Our skeleton army is required for little more than frontier duty and the preservation of forts from decay, with a little fancy duty occasionally in the way of parades.

Richard W. Young.

LEGEND OF MONTROSE.
IN FOUR ACTS.

ACT III.

Three months are supposed to elapse between Acts II and III.

Scene I.—*A cabin used by* Montrose *as a tent during his march from Inverary.*

Sentinels *heard exchanging cries. Distant reveille.*

Discover Montrose *awakening on couch. Knocking heard.*

Montrose. Who comes there, so early?

Enter Angus McAulay.

Angus. 'Tis I, my lord, I have news for you which it is worth your while to rise and listen to.

Montrose. (*Coming forward.*) McAulay can bring no other—are they good or bad?

Angus. As you may decide. Argyle is nearer to our rear than we had imagined. He is moving on Inverlochy with three thousand men, the flower of the sons of Campbell.

Montrose. The voice of McAulay is ever pleasant in the ears of Montrose, and most pleasant when he speaks of some brave enterprise at hand. When will Argyle reach the vale of Inverlochy?

ANGUS. By noon, this very day.

MONTROSE. (*Quickly.*) This day! What are our musters?

ANGUS. About one to their two.

MONTROSE. Then do not hesitate. We will at once to the right-about and countermarch. We, too, can reach Inverlochy by noon, and this shall be a day of battle to us both.

ANGUS. It is gallantly said, my noble lord, and our men were worse than cowards did they not do justice to such a general.

MONTROSE. Let the chiefs and leaders be called together as quickly as possible. We must arrange our plans and decide who best can guide us through these wild mountains the nearest road against our enemy. (*Exit* ANGUS.) So, false Argyle, have we not punished thee enough already? This day decides thy fate and ours. (*Enter* DALGETTY *very ragged,* RANALD, KENNETH.) What, my good friend, Major Dalgetty!

DALGETTY. I pray leave to congratulate you, my most noble general, on the great battles you have achieved since I was detached from you. It was a pretty affair, that march on Inverary, and Argyle has suffered somewhat for infringing the law of arms against my person.

MONTROSE. But where were you, my good Major? We have long given you up for lost.

DALGETTY. It is a long story, my lord, you see—

MONTROSE. Then pray make it short, Major, for pressing matters are at hand.

DALGETTY. Then I may tell you that under heaven, I made my escape by the excellent dexterity which I displayed and by the assistance of this old highlander and his grandson, here.

MONTROSE. A service which shall be requited in the manner it deserves.

DALGETTY. There, you see now it is no small honor to be serving Major Dalgetty. Kneel down, Ranald, kneel down, and kiss his excellency's hand. (RANALD, *with arms folded, makes a low bow only.*)

MONTROSE. What is your name, my friend?

RANALD. It may not be spoken here.

DALGETTY. That is to say, he desires to have his name concealed, in respect he hath in former days, slain certain children, and done other things which, if known, would excite no benevolence among some of your followers. (*Aside to* MONTROSE.) He is an outlaw by profession, and by name called Ranald McEagh. The other is his grandson.

MONTROSE. I understand. These persons are at feud with the McAulays. We will think of the best mode of protecting them. But where have you been, these three months?

DALGETTY. So please your Excellency, I got well out of the castle of Inverary, and would soon have rejoined you; but I was wounded in the pursuit that Argyle gave us. I escaped his clutches through the help of this Highlander and his people, who nursed my wound and have guided me back to my command.

MONTROSE. And you have arrived in good time to be of service, worthy major.

DALGETTY. My lord, in leaving Argyle somewhat suddenly, I failed not to bring with me some tokens of his esteem. Perhaps these papers arrive too late to be of use. (*Hands papers to* MONTROSE *who examines them with eagerness.*) *Aside.*) I will not occupy his valuable time by accounting to him for the gold.

MONTROSE. (*Reading papers.*) Does he not fear me? But he has felt me. He would fire my own castle of Murdoch. I have fired his castle of Inverary. O, for a guide through these passes to Inverlochy!

DALGETTY. If your excellency needs a guide, this poor man, Ranald, knows every pass in the land.

MONTROSE. Indeed! Can you answer for his fidelity?

DALGETTY. I will pledge my pay and arrears, my head and neck, upon his fidelity. A cavalier could say no more for his father.

MONTROSE. We will employ them, but we must have a care against the breaking out of this feud. Let their presence here, and the purpose for which we employ them, be a secret between you and me. [*Exit.*

DALGETTY. Now, you see, friend Ranald, how all goes swimmingly. You will be under my protection and I will take Kenneth to attend my person.

RANALD. You may do so, but lift not your hand upon him; for he is man enough to pay a foot of leathern strap with a yard of tempered steel.

DALGETTY. A most improper vaunt! (*Enter* ALLAN *followed by* ANGUS.) Now, by heaven, here is the very man who will spoil all. ·

ANGUS. You returned, Major, we all thought you dead.

ALLAN. (*Suspiciously.*) Who are these men? .

DALGETTY. This is a—a—Ranald MacGillihuron of Benbecula, who escaped with me out of Argyle's prison; and this is his grandson, Kenneth. Ranald is a harper, and he also hath, like yourself, the capacity of second-sight. (ALLAN *gazes with such intentness on* RANALD *that the latter is about to grasp his dagger, when* ALLAN *extends his hand in friendly greeting.* DALGETTY *watches with great anxiety.*)

ALLAN. You come from the distant island of Benbecula?

DALGETTY. (*Aside.*) Now where is Allan's boasted second-sight that· he cannot tell a deadly enemy from a brother prophet?

ALLAN. (*To* RANALD.) Come hither, come more this way. I would converse with you apart; for men say that in your distant islands the sight is poured forth with more clearness and power than upon us who dwell nearer the Saxons. (*They retire, conversing.*)

DALGETTY. Angus McAulay, when begins the march on Inverlochy?

ANGUS. Within the hour, and I must now see to the safe conveyance of Annot Lyle.

DALGETTY. Annot Lyle! Is she following the campaign.

ANGUS. Surely, we could neither march nor fight, advance nor retreat, without the influence of the Princess of Harps.

DALGETTY. Princess of Harps! Prin-

cess of broadswords and target, I say.

Exeunt ANGUS, DALGETTY, KENNETH.

ALLAN. (*Advancing with* RANALD.) Does the sight come gloomy on your spirits?

RANALD. As dark as the shadow on the moon when she is darkened in her mid-course in heaven, and prophets foretell of evil times.

ALLAN. There is a matter in my visions which greatly perplexes me. Repeatedly have I had the sight of a Highlander who seemed to plunge his weapon into the body of my cousin, Mentieth—

RANALD. (*Aside.*) Mentieth.

ALLAN. The young lieutenant of Montrose. But by no effort, though I have gazed till my eyes were almost fixed in the sockets, can I discover the face of this Highlander, or even conjecture who he may be, although his person and air seem familiar to me.

RANALD. Have you reversed your own plaid, according to the rule of experienced seers in such case?

ALLAN. (*Shuddering.*) I have.

RANALD. And in what guise did the phantom then appear to you?

ALLAN. (*Convulsively.*) With his plaid also reversed.

RANALD. Then be assured that your own hand and none other, will do the deed of which you have witnessed the shadow.

ALLAN. So has my anxious soul a hundred times surmised. But it is impossible! Were I to read the record in the eternal book of fate, I would declare it impossible—we are bound by the ties of blood, and by a hundred ties more intimate—we have stood side by side in battle, and our swords have reeked with the blood of the same enemies—it is IMPOSSIBLE that I should harm him.

RANALD. That you WILL do so is certain. You say (*with emotion*) that side by side you have pursued your prey like bloodhounds—have you never seen bloodhounds turn their fangs against each other, and fight over the body of a throttled deer?

ALLAN. It is false! These are not the forebodings of fate, but the temptation of some evil spirit from the bottomless pit.   [*Exit.*

RANALD. Thou hast it! The barbed arrow is in thy side! Spirits of the slaughtered, rejoice! Soon shall your murderers' swords be dyed in each other's blood.

Martial music at change.

SCENE II.—*A plain near Inverlochy.*

Enter ARGYLE, SIR DUNCAN, NEAL *and* HIGHLANDERS, *armed.*

DUNCAN. I rejoice in the prospect, my lord, that Graham of Montrose will be crushed by none others than us.

ARGYLE. (*His arm is in a sash.*) You are too scrupulous, Sir Duncan. What signifies it by whose hands the blood of Graham is spilt? It is time that that of the sons of Campbell had ceased to flow.

DUNCAN. My lord, my lord, consider that we now have a personal opportunity of settling with Montrose for his depredations. He has left a heavy account in Argyleshire against him, and I long to reckon with him drop of blood for drop of blood.

ARGYLE. How know you that we venture personally with him. James Graham has not ventured to show us his banner.

Distant flourish—Royal salute.

DUNCAN. You may hear, my lord, from yonder signal, that Montrose must be in person among these men.

ARGYLE. (*Timidly.*) And has probably horse with him which we could not have anticipated.

DUNCAN. But shall we look pale for that, my lord, when we have foes to fight and wrongs to revenge?

ARGYLE. Curses on that fall! It was to be that a tumble from my horse should disable me from active service.

DUNCAN. It is true, my Lord of Argyle, you are disabled from using either sword or pistol; you must retire on board the galleys.

ARGYLE. No, it shall never be said that I fled before Montrose; if I cannot fight, I will, at least, die in the midst of my children.

DUNCAN. Nay, my lord, retire; your life is precious to us as a head; your hand cannot be useful to us as a soldier. (*To Neal.*) See him on board, Neal, where he will be in safety. We have other duties to perform. (*Exit* ARGYLE *with* NEAL *and* HIGHLANDERS.) (*Looking after him.*) It is better it should be so, but of his line of a hundred sires, I know not one who would have retired while the banner of Campbell waved in the wind, and in the face of its most inveterate foes.   [*Exit with followers.*

Drums, flourishes, military music at change.

SCENE III.—*Field of Inverlochy. Castle in the distance. Lake and Mountain.*

At change, enter HIGHLANDERS *who come forward and sing:*

BATTLE SONG.

Awake! To arms! To arms! we cry,
  The Campbell banner invites us;
We gain the battle to-day, or die,
  Our deadly enemy fights us.
The terror of war is on the wind,
  And death is hovering o'er us—
But craven the heart of the faltering hind
  That halts in the path before us.

CHORUS.

To arms! Ye Caledonia's sons!
To arms! The lawless foeman comes.
To arms! We fight to save our homes.
  God and the King our cry.

Awake! awake! our foes appear,
  The pibroch's note is sounding;
Our Highland hearts, devoid of fear,
  Exultantly are bounding.
For soon our wrathful arms shall be
  In strife of war engaging,
And naught but death or victory
  Shall stay the battle's raging.—CHORUS.

Enter MONTROSE, MENTIETH, ANGUS, ALLAN, MUSGRAVE, HALL *and followers, armed.*

MENTIETH. (*Looking.*) They are going to put their horses out of danger. Yonder goes Argyle and his men.

MONTROSE. You are wrong, Mentieth, they are saving their precious chief. Give the signal for assault at once—send the word through the ranks. (*Exit two* HIGHLANDERS.) Gentlemen, upon them instantly! [*Exeunt.*

Drums, flourishes, shouts. Enter DAL-GETTY, RANALD. (RANALD *has bows, arrows and broadsword, with target.*)

DALGETTY. Ranald, my trusty comrade, you have no firearms, I dare to aver, and in what manner you propose to do battle, before you come to hand blows, it passeth my apprehension.

During this scene, numbers of HIGH-LANDERS, *arrayed for war, can pass irregularly or in order, hurriedly and with moderate haste. Bagpipes may also be introduced.*

RANALD. (*Showing bow and slapping quiver.*) With the weapons and with the courage of our fathers.

DALGETTY. Bows and arrows! ha, ha, ha! Have we Robin Hood back again? Bows and arrows! ha, ha! Oh, that Dugald Dalgetty should live to see men fight with bows and arrows. Well, Ranald, since they are the word e'en let us make the best of it. Here is game already.

RANALD. (*Drawing Dalgetty.*) Bide we here. See you the glitter of that breastplate. It is Sir Duncan. I (*fighting heard*) will have no hand against him.

Enter SIR DUNCAN, *fighting. Kills soldier, who falls off.*

DALGETTY. Surrender, Sir Duncan and we will give you fair quarter.

DUNCAN. That for your quarter. (*Shoots at* DALGETTY, *who staggers around scarcely knowing whether he is hit or not.* RANALD *throws away bow and attacks* DUNCAN *with sword, cutting him down.*)

Enter ALLAN *and several* HIGHLAND-ERS, *who go to raise* DUNCAN.

ALLAN. Villains! It was my positive orders that Sir Duncan be taken alive Which of you has dared to do this?

RANALD. I have.

ALLAN. Dog of an islander, follow the chase and harm him no farther, unless you mean to die by my hand.

RANALD. That I should die by your hand, red as it is with the blood of my kindred, is not more likely than that you should fall by mine. (*Makes sudden and desperate blow at* ALLAN, *but is successfully parried.*)

ALLAN. (*Astonished.*) Villain, what means this?

RANALD. I am Ranald of the Mist! (*They are about to fight when* DALGETTY *interposes.*)

DALGETTY. Hold up your sword, and prejudice this person no farther, in respect that he is here in my safe conduct.

ALLAN. (*Furiously.*) Fool! stand aside; and dare not come between the tiger and his prey! (*Makes cut at* DAL-GETTY, *who staggers up stage.* RANALD *and* ALLAN *fight.* RANALD *falls wounded and* ALLAN *is about to give the fatal blow.*)

Enter MONTROSE, MENTIETH, ANGUS, MUSGRAVE, HALL, *hastily.*

MONTROSE. For shame, gentlemen, brawling together on so glorious a field of victory. Argyle's forces are completely routed, and the day is altogether ours.

Quick curtain.

END OF ACT III.

AMERICAN INVENTIONS.—An English journal gives credit to Americans for at least fifteen inventions and discoveries which, it says, have been adopted all over the world. First, the cotton-gin; second; the planing machine; third, the mower and reaper; fourth, the rotary printing press; fifth, navigation by steam; sixth, the hot air or caloric engine; seventh, the sewing machine; eighth, the India rubber (vulcanite process) industry; ninth, the machine manufacture of horse shoes; tenth, the sand blast for carving; eleventh, the gauge lathe; twelfth, the grain elevator; thirteenth, artificial ice manufacture on a large scale; fourteenth, the electro-magnet and its practical application; fifteenth, the composing machine for printers.

APOSTASY.

II.

"Now the Spirit speaketh expressly, that in the latter times some shall depart from the faith, giving heed to seducing spirits and doctrines of devils. Speaking lies in hypocrisy; having their conscience seared with a hot iron; forbidding to marry and commanding to abstain from meats." *I Tim., iv: 1—3.*"

A CLERGY which could descend to a mere wrangling after temporal power, and forget or ignore the very spirit of the Gospel whose exponents they were, would hardly fail to partake of the spirit and follow the practices of the infidel nations around them. A primal teaching in the church was that "marriage is honorable in all and the bed undefiled," but three centuries of the Christian era had not passed when restrictions were placed upon matrimony. While marriage was allowed it was discountenanced and celibacy considered more holy and excellent. Those who held such views, many of them, would not yield to the flesh enough to marry, but were 'not above taking to their houses and even beds women who had sworn perpetual chastity, and affirming, most solemnly, there was nothing criminal in this relationship.

After the time of Constantine the vices of the clergy, especially those who officiated in large cities, were augmented in proportion to their honors, wealth, and the favor in which they were held by the emperors. Rites and ceremonies from paganism, undue reverence of martyrs and saints, and respect of relics which began about the fourth century, caused the church to drift farther and farther from the primitive faith and worship. In his history of the fourth century, Mosheim says: "Good men were commingled with bad, yet the number of bad began gradually to increase, so that the truly pious and godly appeared more rare. When the character of most bishops was tarnished with arrogance, luxury, effeminacy, animosity, resentments and other defects; when the lower clergy neglected their proper duties and were more attentive to idle controversy than to the promotion of piety and the instruction of the people; when vast numbers were induced, not by rational conviction, but by fear of punishment and the hope of worldly advantage to enroll themselves as Christians, how can it surprise us that on all sides the vicious appeared a host, and the pious a little band almost overpowered by them? Against the flagitious and those guilty of heinous offences, the same rules of penance were prescribed as before the reign of Constantine; but as the times continually waxed worse, the more honorable and powerful could sin with impunity, and only the poor and unfortunate felt the severity of the laws." (Reid's Mosheim, page 149.)

This is damaging evidence against the claim, made by many, of pure apostolic succession. The apostolic spirit would not and did not remain among those who yielded themselves to every species of luxury and vice, nor was it possible for the power of Christ, Peter or Paul to be transmitted through such a descent. We make more extracts as proof in point. Lord Macaulay, one of the greatest intellects of modern times, has the following to say upon this part of the subject:—"Christianity absorbed and assimilated too much with old pagan rites and ceremonies, and sacrificed much of its own system. It triumphed over Gothic ignorance, Syrian asceticism, Roman policy, and Grecian ingenuity but it retained much of the characteristics of the vanquished, in fact so much, it was no longer the early church."

Our distinguished authority did not assert more than he could prove as may, in part, be seen from the following quotation from Augustine, bishop of Hypps:—"The yoke once laid upon the Jews was more supportable than that laid on many Christians in this age." For the Christian bishops introduced with but slight alterations into the Christian worship, those rites and institutions by which formerly the Greeks and Romans and other nations had manifested their reverence toward their imaginary deities, supposing that the people would more readily embrace Christianity if they perceived the ·rites and symbols handed down to them by their fathers still among the Christians, and saw that Christ and the martyrs were worshiped the same as their Gods and heroes had been. At this time there was of course little difference between the worship of the Christians, and that of the Greeks and Romans. In both of them there were splendid robes, mitres, tiaras, wax tapers, croziers, processions, images, golden and silver vases, and so on *ad infinitum.* The superstitious notions concerning saints, angels and images, which had been continually increasing were very much augmented in the fifth century. The help of departed saints was implored by vast multitudes, and no one tried to check this absurd devotion, nor was there any debate upon the subject as to whether the martyrs had power to intercede in behalf of human affairs.· Disembodied spirits were supposed to be frequent visitors to the spot where their bodies had been buried, and this opinion drew a great conflux of supplicants to the sepulchres of saints. The images of those who had a reputation for sanctity when alive had extraordinary devotions paid them, and many Christians held the same view as pagan priests—that the spirits of departed heroes and saints were present in their images, and that intercession made to an image would receive the same attention as if made directly to the person whom it represented. It had been the custom of pagan priests to have images of their gods and goddesses in their temples, and Christians were not slow to follow the practice, it being introduced by the Cappadocians in the third century. As departed pagan heroes had become deified, so saints and martyrs succeeded in all respects to honors which had been paid the former. The analogy between the two religions made the transition very easy to the bulk of the common ·people. In this as in all

other corruptions the clergy took the lead, not being averse to the pomp and ceremony of paganism, and were particular to accept all the forms of ancient idolatry which would make the transition easier. So close was the resemblance between the two churches, the Christians had the same temples, the same altars and often the same images with the pagans, only giving them new names. Dr. Middleton in his "Letters from Rome," page 160, writes of having seen a statue of a young Bacchus, which was worshiped in the guize of a female saint. Upon page 167 of the same work he says:—"As men are greatly influenced by names, it was even contrived that the name of the new divinity should as much as possible resemble the old one Thus the saint Apollinaris was made to succeed the god Apollo, and St. Martina the god Mars. It was further contrived that, in some cases, the same business should continue to be done in the same place, by substituting for the heathen god a christian saint of a similar character, and distinguished for the same virtues. Thus there being a temple at Rome, in which sickly infants had been usually presented for the cure of their disorders, they found a christian saint who had been famous for the same attention to children; and consecrating the same temple to him, the very same practices are now continued as in the times of paganism." Proof of the great corruption could hardly be stronger than this, but we again quote from authority equally eminent and learned. Dr. Priestly in his "Corruptions of Christianity," vol. I, page 343, says,—"The noblest heathen temple now remaining in the world is the Pantheon or Rotunda at Rome, which as the inscriptions over the portico inform us, having been impiously dedicated of old by Agrippa to Jupiter, and all the gods, was piously reconsecrated by Pope Boniface the fourth to the blessed virgin and all the saints. With this single alteration it serves exactly for all the purposes of the popish, as it did for the pagan worship for which it was built. For as in the old temple every one might find the god of his

11

country, and address himself to that deity to whose religion he was most devoted, so it is the same thing now. Every one chooses the patron whom he loves best; and one may see here different services going on at the same time at different altars, with distinct congregations around them, just as the inclination of the people lead them to the worship of this or that particular saint."

The saints and martyrs being held in such high estimation, as a matter of course, their relics or whatever had been intimately associated with them, came to be highly valued and the priests had an unfailing revenue in selling the bones, dresses, etc., pertaining to their deceased compeers. This foolish practices received its greatest impetus from Gregory the Great in the sixth century, and from Constantine, predecessor of Gregory the second. Upon relic worship, Dr. Priestly has the following to say:—We cannot wonder at the great demand for relics, when we consider the virtues that were ascribed to them by the priests and friars who were the vendors of them in that ignorant age. They pretended they had power to fortify them against temptation, to increase grace and merit, to fright away devils, to still winds and tempests, to secure from thunder, lightning, blasting and all sudden casualties and misfortunes; to stop all infectious disorders, and to cure as many others as any mountebank ever pretended to do." The worship of images met with some opposition but it finally triumphed, assisted materially by the decision of the "Council of Trent," which failed to determine how far the worship should extend, and it was probably carried too far. The following is the decision as found in "Thewall's Idolatry of the Church of Rome," page 382. "On the Invocation, Veneration and Relics of the Saints and on Sacred Images:

"The images, moreover, of Christ and the Virgin Mother of God, and the other saints are to be had and retained, particularly in the churches, and due honor and veneration are to be given to them, not because any divinity or virtue is supposed to reside in them, upon account of which they are to be worshiped; or that any thing is to be sought from them; or that trust is to be placed in images, as was formerly the case among the Gentiles, who placed their trust in idols, but because of the honor which is referred to the prototypes which they represent. So that through the images which we kiss, and before which we uncover our heads and prostrate ourselves, we adore Christ, and we venerate the saints whose similitude they represent, which is sanctioned by the decrees of councils, but especially those of the second Nicene Synod, against the opposers of images." As above inferred the reverence of images was even much greater than allowed by the decision of the council, and the fathers of the church could not but acquiesce in a practice which, in time, became almost universal. At the consecration of images solemn ceremonies were observed and solemn prayers offered up which corresponded closely with solemnities and ceremonies observed by heathens which *they* worshiped as idols. It was wittily observed by a heathen author that the length and solemnity of the consecration depended upon the value of the material used in the manufacture of the image—which is literally true. A solemn consecration, it seems to us, would hardly be necessary if the image was to be simply a remembrance, as it would serve the purpose just as well without a consecration as with it. If an image is a mere representation to refresh the memory, and if there is no real and sacred virtue attached to it, why have there been so many pilgrimages made, at different times, to *particular images*, as for instance to the shrine of St. James, of Compostilla in Spain, and that of our Lady of Loretto of Italy. A whole volume might be written, upon this phase of our subject, showing how literally prophecy has been fulfilled and the law of God transgressed in the worship of wood and stone, to the loss of the spirit of truth, but we have shown enough to prove our point and will forbear, after making one more quotation, and proceed to investigate other corruptions. Dr. Priestly, says:—page 361, volume I,—"At length, therefore Christians came to be idolaters in the same gross sense in which the heathens had ever been, so being equally worshipers both of dead men and their images and bones."

An important, though not a vital principle in the Christian faith was the business of confession. The early Christians were accustomed to have public confession of sins, and when a person had been excommunicated he had to make a public confession of his guilt, before he could be received into the church—the same as now practiced by the Latter-day Saints. The heresies of one generation are the dogmas of the next, and, ere long, auricular was substituted for public confession, and subsequently came the doing of private penance, and the sale of indulgences—another name for the licensing of crime. In the fifth century, Leo the Great gave permission to confess privately to a priest, though the practice of public confession had already fallen into partial disuse. "In this way," says Mosheim, page 197, "the ancient discipline, the sole defence of chastity and modesty was removed and the actions of men were subjected to the scrutiny of the clergy, which was greatly to their interest." Not until the thirteenth century, however, did private confession receive direct pontifical assistance. In the fourth council of the Lateran, A. D. 1215, Innocent III published seventy decrees, and in one of them held it to be an article of faith that every one is bound by a positive and divine ordinance that it is the duty of every one to enumerate and confess his sins to a priest. The same council and the pontiff, denied the conflicting opinions, for some time rife in the church, in relation to transubstantiation, or the presence of real flesh and blood of Christ in the eucharist. The decision was favorable to this strange belief, and subsequently the doctrine of the actual presence became universal in the Romish church.

The sale of indulgences above mentioned, within itself extremely reprehensible, was the means of leading the clergy and priests to the perpetrating of flagrant crimes and horrid blasphemy; and as it was the first prop which Luther endeavored to strike from under the papal chair, we will give the subject more extended notice. Doing of penance first followed auricular confession, and sins might be atoned for by repetitions of the psaltar, bowings, scourgings, alms, pilgrimages, etc. The word indulgence at first meant the relaxation of penance in particular cases, and the penances at first were voluntary, but were finally imposed, and could not be dispensed but by leave of the bishops, who often sold them for immense sums of money. In the twelfth century, the popes, seeing the source of gain to the bishops, limited their power and finally drew the whole sale of indulgences to Rome, and even went so far as to pretend to abolish the punishment due to wickedness in a future state. In 1518 Leo X decreed that the popes had the power to remit both the crime and the punishment of sin, the benefit extending to the dead as well as the living. This Leo had recourse to these indulgences in supplying his exhausted finances. He promised the forgiveness of all sins, past, present and to come, and disposed of his indulgences to whoever would use them, and so they passed from hand to hand—disposed of by common peddlers, who used the artifices of trade to increase the price of them. Texel, a dominican friar, was particularly distinguished for pushing the sale of these indulgences. Among other blasphemous utterances, he promised that if a man had lain with the mother of God, he and the Pope could pardon the crime. He also boasted he had saved more souls from hell with indulgences than had St. Peter with all his preaching. It would be impossible to recite all the blasphemies of which this horrid practice was the cause.

It is revolting to dwell upon such details—the prostitution of power to ends so base and vile. And we are told the spirit of Christ and the Gospel has come from such a source, and that not a link in the chain of succession is lacking to establish the claim of divine authority. The thought is revolting. In truth, the time came long since, when blind lead-ers gave "heed to seducing spirits and doctrines of devils, * * having their conscience seared with a hot iron."

J. L. Robison.

ARCHITECTURE OF COMMON HOUSES.

II.
VENTILATION.

In our last chapter we gave a few hints upon the selection of a site, and the arrangement of rooms for the building of a home. One of the most important things to consider in building a home, is how the building is to be ventilated, and let it be here remarked, that to secure and keep good health, your home must be well ventilated. .

It is estimated by careful investigators that about forty per cent. of all fatal diseases are due to impure air. We think we can stand some bad air, and the way is to attribute death, when it comes, to some disease with another name. But the bad air is the prime cause in a vast number of cases. Carbonic acid by its presence in any quantity indicates a foul state of the air. The normal amount is about seven parts in ten thousand, that is, one cannot breathe more than that without bad effect. The constant need is for pure air. Standing out of doors in ordinary weather, the human body is ventilated each hour by at least one hundred thousand cubic feet of pure air. Indoors every occupied room should have from six hundred to one thousand cubic feet of space to each person there, and at least sixty square feet of room to each, while the air should be so changed by currents as to keep the carbonic acid below eight parts in ten thousand. .

Opportunity for the ingress of pure air, and the egress of that which is impure, is absolutely requisite in the construction of every house. Previous to the introduction of stoves as a warming apparatus for houses, these were moderately well ventilated by the open grate and the fireplaces which they contained. The pure air, because cold, rushed down the chimney, and becoming warm by passing the fire, spread through the house, furnishing life to its inmates. Through the same opening the rarified air, being lightened, ascended, and thus constant renewal was had. In those days ventilation was not studied, because additional means for it were not needed; necessity being the mother of invention, where no necessity existed, means were not considered. Hence in those days ventilation was not discussed; and yet men, and especially women, maintained a degree of health and vigor and hardiness of constitution which are both the marvel and envy of modern times.

Wherein consists the remarkable change since then? Whence the dyspepsia, nervous derangements, consumption, etc., of our times? Through the closing of fire places by the invention of stoves. By this change in household arrangements, the inmates of our houses have been largely deprived of the life-giving oxygen, the vital air of the atmosphere. Every breath we draw, every lamp that burns, every fire that warms us, consumes this air in large quantities; and if it is not replenished by constant ingress from the stores of nature, we must grow dull, pale, weak, inert and finally succumb to disease and death. And yearly, millions go down to untimely graves, and the groans of the dying are constantly heard, as the result of want of ventilation. It has taken a long time for us to learn the fact, and even now it is imperfectly understood.

Houses, then, should be properly ventilated. If no other means have been provided, every window should be arranged with pulleys and fastenings so as to be readily lowered from the top and raised from the bottom. An opening is necessary part of the time, at least, in all weathers, if the room is inhabited. There must be a constant change of air, and this cannot be effected through closed windows and impervious doors.

Pure air is a subject which ought to ·claim the careful attention of every intelligent person. If only a small portion of the attention which we give almost all ordinary wants of life, be given to this all important subject, much of the suffering and sickness might be avoided. It is a well known fact that transoms or fan lights over doors are a certain and safe way of securing good ventilation, and it should always be the aim in building houses, to make provisions for transoms over doors. All systems of ventilation resolve themselves into letting air into a room and pushing air out; and the laws of nature provide for this; but the difficulty lies in securing just the quality of pure air required at any given space, without causing unpleasant draughts.

Up to the present there have been two modes of ventilation suggested. First, where the inlet is from above and the outlet below, and, second, where the inlet is from below and the outlet above. It is evident the first method is based on the idea that the rarefied air will first ascend to the top of the apartment, where it will cool and then descend, forcing out the vitiated air previously cooled. The objections to this system are that the carbolic acid and vapor from the body and lungs being specifically lighter than the air in the room will naturally ascend, and by gradually mixing with the pure air as it flows in, will necessarily vitiate it and in descending will be respired in this condition.

The most usual mode of practicing the second system whether in connection with warming or not has been to admit the pure air from below, and expel it from above. This is an obvious mode of ventilating, which is daily illustrated by a window open at top and bottom, when it will be found the air enters the room from below, and goes out from above; or by an open door, where by holding a light it will be seen that the flame is forced inward when held near the floor, and outward when held near the top of the door. This system, however, is not perfect, as it has failed in many instances, owing, no doubt, to local and atmospheric conditions. There are two other systems that are sometimes used, but their costliness precludes them from ever coming into general use. These systems have to be operated by special machinery, and we will not treat on them in connection with the ventilation of common homes.

Great care should be exercised in the ventilation of bed rooms, as it has been calculated that over one-third of our lives are passed in them. The following is one of the best and simplest modes of securing ventilation of bed rooms, and it has never been known to fail: a piece of wood three inches high, and exactly as long as the breadth of the window is to be prepared. Let the sash be now raised, the slip of wood placed on the sill, and the sash drawn closely upon it. If the slip has been well fitted, there will be no draught in consequence of this displacement of the sash at its lower part, but the top of the lower sash will overlap the bottom of the upper one, and between the two bars perpendicular currents of air not felt as draft will enter and leave the room.

In the kitchens the usual way to secure proper ventilation at all times, is the making of a flue near the smoke flue, and connected on the outside by caps. In this manner the heat from the smoke flue furnishes proper draught for the carrying off of all odors, resulting from cooking, etc.

There are hundreds of houses in the country that are built over dark, noisome holes full of dampness, impure air, decaying vegetables and rotting timbers. These holes in the ground are called cellars, but they are so unsuited for the purposes for which they are designed to serve, that they deserve rather to be called "death-traps." Light is as essential to the healthiness and purity of a cellar as it is to the dining room or parlor. The requisites of a good cellar are, freedom from dampness, light and a temperature low enough to prevent decay, and there is no difficulty in securing these conditions if proper care is taken. Plenty of light should be secured for all rooms. A dark house is always unhealthy. Want of light stops growth, and promotes scrofula, rickets, etc., among children. People lose their health in a dark house, and if they get ill they cannot get well again in it. The action of light tends to develop the different parts of the body in just proportions which characterize the species. In warm climates the exposure of the whole surface of the body to the action of light has been observed to be very favorable to the regular conformation of the body. Humboldt confirms this in the account of his voyage to the equinoctial regions. He says: "Both men and women (whose bodies are constantly inured to the effects of light) are very muscular, and possess fleshy and rounded forms. It is needless to add that I have not seen among this people a single case of natural deformity." Let daylight shine through your house without let or hindrance. Let carpets and curtains fade rather than those who occupy the house. Windows should be large and airy, and it will be much better to have the glass bill count up than to spend the same for iron in the shape of tonics. Every nook and corner should have light at least during some part of the day. Health is the most important object to be attained in the construction of our dwellings. Dr. Johnson says: "To preserve health is a moral and religious duty, for health is the basis of all social virtues. We can be useful no longer than we are well." Perhaps the most essential agents of health are proper heating and good ventilation. Modern improvements are excellent things until used in excess, when they become more troublesome than useful. This is especially true of heating. The great number of stoves now on the market show what progress has been made during the last few years, to furnish heat for our dwellings, but stoves are unhealthy when not properly taken care of. The danger from the cast-iron stove is in its weakness not in its strength, for you may fill a room with air, every mouthful of which has passed between red hot iron plates, and the essential properties of the air will not hurt when properly cooled. Carbon which is thrown off from an iron stove is not poison. But trying to breathe it in large quantities will strangle you. But carbonic acid, which is also liberated from burning coal is an active poison, and one per cent. of it in the air we breathe may prove fatal. All stoves for heating should be so constructed that all foul air may be carried off as soon as formed and fresh air supplied in its place, and great care ought to be exercised in selecting heating stoves. Steam heating is coming largely in fashion, but the great expense incurred in introducing it, prevents its use in the majority of houses.

To secure a happy home, one must be careful to study the effects of ventilation, light and heating, as these things alone are the most important points for health, happiness and old age. In our next we will endeavor to point out helps in furnishing a home to suit the requirements of all.   *W. S. Hedges.*

LIFE ON THE INDIAN RESERVATIONS.

II.

THE long controversy in Congress and in most of the States over the right of the Indians to establish independent governments within the confines of the States—as they had done in Georgia and Alabama—resulted, May, 1830, in the passage of a national law "providing for the exchange of lands with the Indians within any of the States or Territories, and for their removal west of the river Mississippi."

"The first section authorized the President of the United States to cause so much of any territory belonging to the United States, west of the river Mississippi, and not included in any State or organized Territory, and to which the original Indian title was extinguished, as he might judge necessary, to be divided into a suitable number of districts, for the reception of such tribes or nations of Indians as may choose to exchange the lands where they now reside, and remove to the west.

"The second section authorized the President to exchange the lands embraced in any such districts with any tribe or nation of Indians then residing within the limits of any of the States or Territories, for the land claimed and occupied by them within such States or Territories.

"The third section authorized the President to *solemnly* assure the tribes with whom the exchange was made, that the United States would *forever* secure and guarantee to them and their heirs or successors, the country so exchanged with them, and, if they prefer it, the United States would cause a patent or grant to be made and executed to them for the same.

"The fourth section authorized the President to ascertain such improvements on the lands of the Indians as added value to the same, and cause such value to be appraised, and to pay the amount of the same to the parties rightfully claiming such improvements.

"The fifth section authorized the President to render such aid as was necessary and proper, to enable the emigrants to remove to and settle in their new home; and such aid as was necessary for their support for one year after their removal.

"The sixth section authorized the President to cause each tribe that emigrated to be protected at their new residence, against all interruption or disturbance from any other tribe of Indians, or from any other person or persons whatever.

"The seventh section provided for the same superintendence and care in their new home that was extended to them where they then resided.

"The eighth and last section appropriated the sum of five hundred thousand dollars to enable the President to give effect to the law."

This was the beginning of the reservation system as we are familiar with it now. But from its adoption, notwithstanding the solemn assurance of the United States that the limits of the Indian's territory should not be reduced, there has in reality been no interruption in the course pursued in the beginning, followed during all the years since the whites came to America and that is still in fashion, of crowding the red man oft his lands as soon as they become desirable in the eyes of the superior race. Only last summer the doctrine was reiterated by Senator Logan, chairman of the committee on Indian affairs. The committee was on a tour of inspection of the Indian agencies, a duty performed at the Crow agency in the following manner: The agent was duly apprized of the intended visit and had arrangements made for the transportation from the nearest railway station, of the distinguished gentlemen comprising it, viz: Senators Logan, Cameron, Dawes and suite. The agency buildings were cleaned up, beds prepared and the government attachés of the reservation on hand to do honor to the occasion. A council of the chiefs was called as it was understood that a proposition would be made by the Great Father to cut down the Crow reservation and throw open to the white settlers and ranchers the magnificent grazing region, lying between the Boulder Creek, the present western limit, and the Big Horn River, a reduction of nearly seventy per cent. The committee left its special palace car and drove over to the agency, a distance of eighteen miles, in the morning, and immediately on arrival went into council with the chiefs. The council lasted nearly two hours during which the elaborate preparations for dinner were completed.

On the breaking up of the council, which had been most unsatisfactory, the Indians positively refusing to consider any new proposition to cede their territory until the conditions of their last previous treaty were fulfilled by the government, Senator Logan, speaking very hotly, ordered the teams; said there was no use talking with such men, and that if they wouldn't consent to the cession willingly, they must be made to. He and the others then entered the carriages, drove back to their palace car, discussed the good cheer its larder afforded, and left the Crows, agency, Indians and treaty, greatly honored, but awfully disappointed, to be at some time remembered in the preparation of a report to the Senate, which we shall read with interest when it appears. The visit of inspection occupied two hours and forty minutes; and we have reason to suppose that it was a fair average visit, such as Senate and House committees usually pay. As a matter of fact the Indian, his interests and rights and claims upon the government, are barely alluded to, consideration of such questions being universally deferred until the legislators return to Washington and are surrounded by the land-grabbers and speculators, whose influence is the ever potent power that issues and enforces the command to the poor Indian: "Red man, move on !"

The "home work" on each reservation, comprises the missionary and educational labor performed. This at the Crow agency is remarkable only in the reports of the agent and in the little mind of the Methodist minister employed there at government charge. Ostensibly a school is kept for the benefit of Indian children, who are supposed to be taught the rudiments of English, and religious services are held to promote the Christian faith among the degenerate savages. The facts on the Little Rosebud agency are that the religious services are confined exclusively to the comforting of the little band of Methodists, who hold all the government offices there, and but for the offices would not be there, nor in any other Indian country. The school is kept to teach *their* children, and if any good Indian should profess to be con-

verted to Methodism, *his* children also attend. In this way *twelve Indian children* have been enrolled as pupils. The population of the agency is thirty-five hundred, and at least one fifth, children of school age. There is a little farming done; under the direction of a paid instructor of agriculture. . Altogether *thirty* Indians have been induced to engage in this civilizing pastime, and the fruit of their labors as seen in the growing fields, is the most satisfactory of any produced on the reservation, unless we except the stock raising by the "squaw men."

This is the most important from a commercial standpoint. No better range for cattle exists in the world than that of the Crow reservation. The luxuriant mountain grass grows so thickly as to cover the rolling hillsides and lovely valleys, the broad tablelands and river bottoms with a verdant mat of nutritious food, affording provender summer and winter to thousands of cattle, and ever tempting the greed of the white man, who would like to herd his own droves there. To accomplish this—the sordid love of gold is so much greater than self-respect or honor—white men sometimes marry Indian women, and this fact admits them to the reservation as residents, and secures them equal rights with the Indians to the use of the range, the streams and the game. They are called "squaw men," who thus shield themselves in the bosoms of Indian women to rob the fallen race of the few remaining privileges they enjoy. One of these, it was reported to us, formed such a connection six years before, when he was worthless, having lost a fortune, with nothing left but a few cows and an ardent admiration for the finest looking squaw on the reservation. Last spring he sold out his stock herds, and netted forty thousand dollars, which he continues to enjoy in the society of his red wife and several little half-breed papooses.

The trader on the reservation, in the course of a few years, becomes wealthy. He buys at ridiculously low prices, always paying in goods out of the store at equally absurd high prices, the robes, furs and skins of the Indians. These are bound in bundles and shipped to Chicago and the east, where good prices are received, especially for buffalo robes. As the buffalo becomes scarce, its robe is more sought after and commands better prices, thus we were informed that fine four year old cow robes, Indian tanned, will readily fetch from fifteen to twenty dollars in New York. Such robes are bought of the Indians for from four to six dollars in store goods, and are sold at retail by the traders to occasional visitors, such as we were, at from eight to twelve dollars, cash. A universal characteristic of the men we saw about the agencies is their utter indifference to the rights of the Indian. When they consider him with favor it is by condescension, not that he has a just claim for consideration upon them. There is occasionally to be observed a friendly interest in certain favorites, who become such from the accommodation or profit they may render the agents or their associates. But a genuine regard for the rights and welfare of the Indians is rarely met.

De Vallibus.

THE POET'S PASSION.

How distant often seems what is beloved,
When silent worship is the highest key;
Who hath not by this real of life been moved,
A memory of the past—or yet to be?

Not by the forms we see e'en now and then,
Whose surface, contour, may arrest the sight;
Oh, things may be quite fair to common ken,
And yet lack soul which thrills like song at night!

The landscape may be lovely as a dream,
Its harmonies as if of Paradise;
And one will catch, ah, e'en its brightest gleam,
When to another, it is simply—nice!

The sculptor's art from marble may evoke
True inspiration bursting to his will;
What patient toil, what touch, what artist stroke,
But to the soulless, it is marble still!

Tell all the masters who have pencil used,
And on the canvas bid their thought to swell;
Till 'rapt souls gaze as if themselves transfused,
But millions simply ask, "Why, will it sell?"

So if 'tis music, glorious and sublime,
Echoes from far, of symphonies above,
And then rehearsed by gifted men in Time,
Are there not querists, "What doth music prove?"

Oh dull, uncomprehending mortals we,
Sightless to beauty, to its glory dead;
Or if 'tis visible, but gold most see,
And barter turns it into paltry lead!

Yet beauty is, its ideals grace the world,
Itself hath beauty 'neath its varied skies;

And oft the human soul hath half unfurled,
Trophies of labor, skill, which heaven doth prize.

But all these seemings, landscape as it is,
Man's art, his science, music, painting, all,
Are nothing to the glory which is his,
As man, as woman, where there is a soul!

What gulfs between, how one illumined lives,
Another, sordid, nearly void of good;
Light, love, and blessing is the wealth he gives,
While death, not life, the other understood.

In woman, sunshine from the soul steals out,
With beauty glorified a queen she stands,
Or, like a meteor as it sweeps about,
No good distilling from her outstretched hands.

Worship instinctive give we to the true,
And at a distance love or homage pay;
'Tis soul, not form, the first is ever new,
The latter vanisheth within a day.

Soul is immortal, beauty is its dress,
Its own expression, without counterfeit;
Time and Eternity but this express,
Perfection's stamp, is Heaven's ideal yet.

Silence befits the poet, yet for speech
He waits in patience till the influx swells,
Till eloquence can his ideal reach,
Then his vocation in his music tells.

Oh beauty, soulful beauty be to me
The glimpse of heaven, assurance of its truth;
The dream of life, the is—and yet to be—
God's welcome promise of eternal youth!

H. W. Naisbitt.

THE CONTRIBUTOR.

A MONTHLY MAGAZINE.

JUNIUS F. WELLS,
EDITOR AND PUBLISHER.

TERMS:
Two Dollars a Year,   *In Advance.*

SALT LAKE CITY,   AUGUST, 1884.

WILLIAM W. TAYLOR.

WE are called again to mourn the loss of a friend and brother, whose association has been to those best acquainted with him a source of the greatest pleasure and comfort; whose agreeable disposition made him one of the most lovable of men, and whose splendid character won from all who met him the sincerest respect. Elder William W. Taylor, though but thirty years of age at the time of his death, had already made for himself a name that will long be remembered and cherished by those among whom he lived and labored. Early in life he displayed the rare qualities of head and heart that lie at the foundation of a great man's career. He was in a remarkable degree a lover of truth and all principles of probity and honor for their own sake. To him there was no greater pleasure than the practice of those principles, and he rarely if ever lost an opportunity of proving his devotion to them. The instance quoted in the editorial of the *Deseret News* of his absolute fidelity to principles of honor serves as an illustration of his life's practice and as an example of his teachings to his fellow men: "When a mere boy, he with a companion went to the old adobe yard, where a skating pond had been prepared, for entering which a charge of twenty-five cents was made. William and his friend were anxious to get on the pond to skate, but they had no money. They succeeded, however, without the knowledge of the proprietor, in effecting an entrance. When William thought of what he had done, he felt condemned, and to satisfy his conscience resolved to repay the man with the first money he could earn. He earned a dollar, and he immediately took it to him and insisted upon his taking a four-fold payment for the wrong he had done him."

William Whittaker Taylor, the son of President John Taylor and Harriet Whittaker Taylor, was born September 11, 1853, in the Fourteenth Ward, Salt Lake City, Utah. He resided in the same Ward all his life, and was never absent from the Territory, except on brief visits, with the exception of the time spent upon a mission to Great Britain. During his school days, and at a very early age in life Brother Taylor evinced strong religious convictions and a desire to be useful in the work of the ministry. Thus at an age quite unusual, he became a teacher in the Sabbath school, and performed the duties of Teacher in the Ward for several years, before being called to go upon his mission abroad. He was also chosen by Elder Edward W. Davis and regularly sustained by the general conference as first counselor in the presidency of the Elders' quorum, an office which he faithfully filled to the satisfaction of his brethren. It was in this office and while attending the meetings of the Elders' quorum in the years 1874-5, that we became personally acquainted with Brother William, and formed a friendship that has been constant and to us one of the most gratifying and profitable of our lives.

At the October conference, 1875, Elder Taylor was called to go upon a mission to Great Britain, leaving home on the 26th of that month. He spent nearly two years abroad, returning October 16, 1877, during which the duties of a missionary, a messenger of life and salvation, were performed with that zeal and energy which was characteristic of him in all his labors. He won the esteem of the Saints abroad, and was a favorite among the Elders associated with him. No blemish attached to his ministry among the people there, and he bore to them a faithful testimony, warning the wicked and teaching them repentance, while comforting the faithful with words of encouragement and an example of purity and integrity that is remembered by them and has its influence to this day, and will for all time to come.

On returning home he was appointed clerk of the High Council of Salt Lake Stake of Zion, and was sustained as a home missionary in the Stake. The laborious duties of the former office were well and carefully performed, though often requiring him to labor long hours both day and night, the sessions of the High Council generally being in the evening and frequently lasting until midnight. In recording the proceedings of these Councils and taking the minutes of Stake conferences, missionary and quorum meetings, etc., he became an expert, and leaves lasting evidence of his capability, in this respect, in the carefully preserved records made by him.

In April, 1880, Brother Taylor was chosen to be one of the First Seven Presidents of the Seventies, succeeding in that office Elder A. P. Rockwood, deceased. To his careful attention and indefatigable labor may be fairly ascribed much of the success that has attended the local organizations of the Seventies, brought about since the instructions were received to fill the quorums and put them in order. He was well adapted for this work and will be remembered for his assiduous connection with it.

In political matters, Brother William had, for one of his age, unusual experience, having attended many conventions, labored several times as an officer of the Territorial Legislative Assembly, and at its last session, as a member of the Council, in which capacity he displayed excellent judgment and rendered most satisfactory service to his constituents. He was elected last February to the office of Assessor and Collector of Salt Lake City, which office he held at the time of his death. On the Saturday previous to his demise, he performed the last public labor of his life, as delegate to the convention for the nomination of county officers.

On Tuesday morning, August 5, 1884, at 4 o'clock, Brother William peacefully passed away. He had been confined to his bed but a few days, and his sufferings were not prolonged, but from the beginning of his illness he had no faith that he would recover. Prest. George Q. Cannon and other brethren administered to him and seemed to have strong testimony that their prayers would avail, but it was ordered otherwise, and his noble spirit, called to a higher sphere, could not be retained on earth.

"In the morning of his days, in the midst of a career of great usefulness, at a time when his services were in great demand here, and when his future earthly life appeared full of bright promise, he has been called away to labor in a higher and more ·extended sphere. His family and friends and associates will miss him. Their grief is profound, and would be inconsolable if it were not for the promise and comforting hopes of the Gospel. That glorious plan, however, assures us that in leaving this state of existence, he goes to enter upon a better one, and that there he will find opportunity for the fullest exercise of the choicest qualities which made him so loving and attractive while here. That God who gave him life has seen fit to call him hence, and it is for us who remain to bow in humble submission to the will of Him who rules both in heaven and on earth, and will in all eternity."

FISH LAKE.

THIS beautiful sheet of water lies in Sevier County, at the very summit of the Wasatch range, ten miles east of Koosharem, Grass Valley, and at an elevation of about ten thousand feet above sea level. Leaving the Sevier Valley at Rocky Point above Salina, the road takes a south-easterly direction, winding for several miles through a series of elevations much resembling immense mole hills overlapping one another, tinted with almost every color of the rainbow, and sparsely covered with scrub cedar in every stage of growth and decay. It is therefore with a feeling of relief that the eye rests, in this parched region, upon a green valley known as King's Meadows. It is evening, and the shadows begin to merge into one general shade. Before us, as we arrive, lies the verdant green, dotted by covered wagons and tents. Nearer are the horses contentedly grazing, while in the distance, around blazing camp fires, we catch the radiant faces and hear the merry chat of excursionists who have arrived before us. It was here, at a recent date under the stars of heaven, that President Woodruff and Brother Wheelock, veterans of the Nauvoo exodus, recounted to a multitude of our mountain youths there assembled in a circle, the wonderful scenes of Zion's Camp, and recalled predictions concerning the future of God's kingdom, made by the Prophet in their hearing that they had seen literally fulfilled, and others so grand that even they could scarcely comprehend their fulfilment.

A three hours' drive the next morning through a canyon thickly wooded with pitch pines and cedars which are being utilized by charcoal burners, brings us into an open rolling country appropriately named Grass Valley. One thing that strikes us besides the abundance of forage lining the gently sloping hillsides is the conspicuous absence of cattle, which, a few years ago, roamed in thousands over the verdant valley. As we descend the sloping grade, our eyes catch sight of a number of white specks on the opposite side of the valley, slowly crawling in line up the steep mountain side. But as we are out to view the beauties of nature, we must not forget to notice the lovely rivulet now almost at our feet. Who would think that this clear, limpid stream gliding noiselessly its serpentine course between mossy banks and through green meadows— should form part of that muddy, turbulent Sevier, which, controlled, makes thousands of smiling fields and homes,

but which, uncontrolled, rushes on carrying destruction in its path? A picture of infancy and after life.

We are now to the top of the mountain. The hardy pitch-pines and cedars are replaced by the more graceful quaking asp, balsam and timber pines. The grasses and flowers, in the valley long ago withered and dried, here, following close upon the heels of the melting snow drifts, stand out in their gayest attire, the one adorning the other like gems sparkling from a velvet-green setting. The air, sultry and loaded with dust in the valley, has suddenly changed to a fresh, cool, invigorating breeze that makes one wish his lungs were larger.

A few miles more of undulating country—basin-shaped valleys whose centres contain miniature lakes encircled by belts of meadow grass, and whose sides are dotted in places by isolated quaking asp groves that break ground nearer and nearer the water's edge each year —brings us to the wonder of wonders; but before starting let us take a retrospective view of the valley we have just left. Wonderland! There lying before us is the joint product of nature and art—the tesselated fields. The grain varying in color from a light yellow to a dark green, makes a beautiful contrast with the brown, summer-fallowed squares interspersed; and as every creek, road or other division is sharply defined, the whole has the appearance of a checker board, except that the spots are infinitely more varied. Truly what is common-place in the foreground becomes beautiful in the perspective. How true this is of life, when old age is the foreground and childhood the perspective!

But to stop philosophizing, let us continue our journey, and instead of taking the mainly traveled road seek some eminence from which the anticipated scene shall burst upon us at once. Here we are at the top of the mountain to the west. Beneath us a few feet lies a large snow bank slowly "leaking away its life." A short distance beyond peep from luxuriant vegetation the bluebell and larkspur. One thousand feet below and scarcely twice that distance away, lies the chief of our mountain scenery, Fish Lake. A slight breeze ruffles its surface into ten thousand mirrors, sparkling in the sunshine. It is hemmed in on almost every side by a graceful rim of quaking asp trees, which, on its eastern shore, uncovered by foliage and shrubbery usually skirting the water's edge, and as if marshaled into line, expose their bold nakedness for nearly its entire length of seven miles. A few feet in the background tower the less graceful but sturdier firs and pines, lining a mountainside so steep that one imagines he could touch their tops when standing on the the ground above. On the western side we notice a curious feature, which we shall examine more closely when we take an excursion on the lake. It is a sort of dyke or embankment thrown up by nature or art wherever the water would naturally form an inlet or bay. Thus while the circular form of the lake is preserved, it is at the same time separated in places from the small meadow plats thus formed by a trellis work of trees and underbrush growing on the embankment.

On both the eastern and the western sides, at intervals of half a mile, extend groves of quaking asp, willow and birch, their cones reaching far up the mountain sides, and betokening the birth of as many babbling brooks, incessantly making music to the gambols of the trout that seek their playful freshness during the spawning season. The wind has ceased, and the lake lies before us a motionless sea of glass. Crystal Mirror would be a more appropriate name, lovers of fish to the contrary, notwithstanding. Even at this distance the bottom is plainly visible: First a broad belt of brownish-red, then a smaller one of burnished silver, succeeded by one of gray, gradually merging into a deep blue, while on the other side as the lightest breath of air finds its way through the tall trees and strikes the surface, the color is changed to a dark green. What causes these changes of color? We shall see, presently. We are now descending the mountain-side, and as we

follow the windings of the galloping stream, it may not be uninteresting to note the dewy depths of the surrounding vegetation, as they smile forth, from fragrant bosoms, health and happiness to the beholder; or to pass the hand over the velvet moss on the log fallen athwart the stream, where the cool, sprinkling spray keeps it moist; or even to let the eye penetrate the shady depths of a nook in the stream where, protected by overhanging birch-roots, the wary trout deposit their spawn.

But we are now to the lake shore, and before embarking on the raft lying yonder, let us examine this curious levee. Can it be that the ancient Nephites also made excursions to this beautiful vale, and that it is the work of their hands, or has it been from time immemorial, as it is at the present, the fishing ground of their dusky brethren? Or is it but a freak of nature? It seems too regular and studied for the fantastic whims of this dame. It is about six feet wide on the top, varying in height from four to ten feet, and everywhere made of the same material—a conglomerate of earth and boulders, the latter, protruding, still almost hidden by creeping vines, growing out of the crevices. The most plausible theory is advanced by Messrs. Spencer, Madsen and Stevenson, who, at different seasons, have made this peculiar feature a careful study. They declare that boulders rolling from the mountain-sides lodge in the shallow water skirting the shore. The ice breaking up in the spring is driven by the waves with irresistible force, carrying the boulders before it to low water mark. Sand and gravel are scooped up in the same way. The bulwark thus formed is raised a little each year by the expanding force of the ice pressing against it, while new deposits are left on top by melting heaps of ice, whose undersides, lying in winter close upon the bottom, have imbedded in them sand and gravel.

We push our rude craft out upon the still, clear water, and observe that the red belt before alluded to, now takes the definite shape of numberless sub-aqueous plants. Detaching a few with our guiding poles, we notice that, fern-shaped, they grow here from four inches to a foot, culminating in a tassel gradually changing in color from a dark brown to a maroon. The shining rim fringing the red is nothing more than the glimmering of sand and gravel marking the descent of a submarine terrace. The water now becomes deeper and vegetation more luxuriant. Other plants are added: one whose leaves very much resemble those of the pine; another, a kind of grass, grows ten feet long, gently spreading in wavy folds upon the ground. A thrust of the pole to the bottom reveals the fact that the vegetation here forms a mat three feet thick, and from its peculiar smell, we judge that there underneath must be the land of fish. The bottom is now about twenty-five or thirty feet deep, and we paddle our way to reach the blue line. Suddenly, within an oar's length, the bottom vanishes from our sight, and we conclude that here must be a "jump off," and begin to speculate about the origin of this novel freak of nature. From the narrowness of its northern end (a few hundred yards), and the wideness of its southern (about a mile and a half), together with the general trend of the adjoining ravines, we conclude that this was once a large canyon. A landslide, damming up its mouth, compelled the imprisoned water to flow from what was before its source, forming as it now does the source of the Dirty Devil River. There are also good grounds for attributing to it a volcanic origin. A high mountain terminating abruptly in the north end of the valley, suggests the idea that what was once its continuation has, by an earthquake, been suddenly rent in twain, leaving the chasm now occupied by the lake.

THE CONFERENCE.

As most of our readers will already have learned, the occasion of so general an excursion to Fish Lake was the Young Men's Mutual Improvement Association Conference of Sevier Stake. A spacious bowery, built a year ago by the enterprising brethren of the adjacent villages, on an open eminence overlooking the lake from the northwest, had already been refitted. The road formerly following the inside edge of the embankment, where the water was no deeper than to the hubs of the vehicles, was this year impracticable, owing to the increased depth of the lake. A new road and dugway, costing upwards of two hundred dollars, was therefore cut through the groves along the western mountain side by members of the Young Men's Association of the adjoining settlements. The attendance was large, there being upwards of six hundred people present. Besides President Woodruff and Elder Joseph A. West, of the General Superintendency, no less than seventeen of the eighteen ward associations were represented, including all the Stake officers.

There were present of the Stake fourteen Bishops and their Counselors, together with the Stake Presidency—a feature alike pleasing and encouraging to the young men, and one that might be emulated in some other Stakes. The reports, both verbal and statistical, were very favorable; and from the latter we gathered the following interesting items: Of eight hundred and seventy-five young men in the Stake, seven hundred and thirty-seven, or nearly eighty-four per cent. are members of the Associations, while a large number of the non-members are regular attendants, who, through fear of having appointments given them, do not enter their names. Of eighteen Associations, seventeen issue manuscript papers, thus giving great opportunity for cultivating the art of writing. The conference throughout was replete with good instruction and wise counsel to the young, given by Presidents Woodruff, Spencer, Thurber, Seegmiller, Elders Wheelock, Palmer, West, Sisters Horne and Richards, and others; and while the closest digest would swell this sketch to undue proportions, I cannot refrain from presenting a few of the leading points: Brother West, commenting on the fact that frequently young men, on taking up subjects to speak, began by explaining that they had not prepared their subject, preferring rather to let the Spirit enlighten their minds, and quoting, as a reason, Christ's saying: "Take no thought about what ye shall say," etc.; stated that this was a wrong interpretation, for we are enjoined to seek information from all good and useful books, and we should therefore get information on a subject from every source. It is the office of the Holy Ghost to arrange this information —to *bring to the mind* things past, present, and reveal things to come. But how is it possible to bring to mind anything that has not been stored there? The caution of our Savior was not intended to discourage research, but to prevent the learning by rote, sectarian fashion, of parrot-like speeches. This view was corroborated by President Woodruff and other speakers following.

On the subject of the relation of the sexes, President Woodruff said that virtue reigns in Zion, and herein lies her strength. Every young woman of Israel has the right to expect perfectly honorable, respectful treatment from the young men of Zion, whose virtue should be as dear to them as that of their sisters. Young men, study all good books, but especially the Scriptures. If you do not see the force of this counsel now, you will see it with regret when you have been called on missions. From the ranks of the young men of these mountains must rise the rulers of the world. This kingdom will ultimately triumph over all others; not by the sword, but by the power of Truth and the favor of Almighty God. The Prophet Joseph and the Apostles will judge this generation. Every man and boy will be held responsible for the Priesthood he receives, for it is a power given to man only to glorify God.

THE CAMP.

This sketch would yet be incomplete without a picture of our camping ground and amusements. After meeting, Saturday, the martial band was discoursing some lively music, and Brother Thurber, with his usual tact for sport, stalking back and forth with his gun, military fashion, soon inspired the company with a desire to march. Falling into procession, and following the band, over which waved the stars and stripes, we made a wide circuit of the camp, and after cutting several curious figures on the greensward, were wheeled into a circle. "Halt," cried our captain, as he brandished aloft his sword (a quaking asp pole). "I propose a stump speech by Brother Bagley." This was loudly seconded by the whole company and happily responded to. In the midst of the applause following the grandiloquent oration, came the command, "Silence!" Again ascended the knotty sword: "I now propose three cheers for Zion." The long pent-up feelings of the multitude found voice, and the echoing hills reverberated their gladness. We then assembled around President Woodruff's headquarters, and after singing "The Spirit of God like a fire is burning," and never before have I heard it come from so near the heart, President Woodruff pronounced the evening benediction, and, by request, recited some of the stirring episodes of Zion's Camp, after which the company dispersed to their several quarters.

It is dusk, and as we sit making pictures in the blazing fire, we are suddenly aroused from our reverie by the falling of a log eaten in two by the flames. We now begin to realize the novelty of our situation. Before us, their hands behind them, palms to the fire, stand a few of the veterans of earlier days, the radiating rays glistening upon their silvery locks and revealing the broad backs and stooping forms bent under the loads of care that must soon fall upon younger shoulders. A moment's listening suffices to convince us that they are drawing from the store of memory on the only subject that would be suggested to them by the camp fire and President Woodruff's late reminiscences — early times. Following the departing rays in another direction, our eye falls upon the broad, white canvas, while, underneath, the playful beams darting from spoke to spoke, descry to us the dim, shadowy outlines of frying-pans, camp kettles and other cooking utensils. A slight breeze is blowing from the lake, and we hear the tiny waves musically kissing the pebbles on the shore. From the grassy hillside and sloping plain on the north come to our ears the sounds of various bells; some discordant, regular, others musical, while the most melodious are those coming from so great a distance that we catch but an occasional tinkle as the wind changes. And now comes a ringing winnow which seems to say, "I've lost my mate," for in a moment is heard the answer in a different inflection,"Here I am." Following a succession of dull thuds, as of something striking the earth at regular intervals, Frank, the sturdy old horse, hobbled, pushes his head and shoulders out of the darkness from between the wagons, and, staring with both eyes and ears, announces his arrival with a short neigh, which, translated, means, "It is time for grain."

But our description refers to only one of the many camps forming this interesting group; let us, therefore, take a more comprehensive view. What an illumination! A hundred fires gleaming from the edge of a semi-circular grove,and lighting up at the same instant, in various shades,wagons, tents, trees and people; while around a blazing fire in an open space in the centre, lazily lounge a group of Indians, some standing, some lying upon the ground, all alternately turning their cold sides to the fire. The sounds striking the ear are about as varied as the component parts of the panoramic view before us. On making a tour of the encampment, we discover the old folks quietly taking their rest, and the young people hurrying to another part of the grove, where blazing fires have been kindled. On our way thither, we encounter the sign, "Ice Cream," and conclude, as we button more tightly our overcoats, that while the latter article is always good, Nature will furnish plenty of the former on our camp kettles before morning. We are now in the midst of gay groups of young men and ladies seated in different circles that vie with one another in songs, toasts and recitations, while in another circle the martial band is doing its best

to enliven this the last night in the woods.

Such, then, is a meagre, a very imperfect description of *one* trip to the mountains. For outdoor conferences, we have only words of commendation. We need not all journey to Fish Lake, for nearly every canyon traversed by a mountain stream presents almost equal attractions. Why not enjoy, then, what is legitimately ours—the cool, crystal water, the health-giving verdure, the pure, bracing atmosphere; forget awhile the cares of life and place ourselves in sweet communion with Nature and with Nature's God?   *N. L. Nelson.*

PUBLICATIONS RECEIVED.

PICTORIAL BIBLE AND COMMENTATOR FOR YOUNG PEOPLE, by Ingram Cobbin, V. D. M. Agent for Utah, R. S. Horne.

THE above work is one that promises to have a large sale in this Territory, meeting as it does with general favor of Bible students and instructors. It is written in familiar narrative style and conveys in great simplicity the lessons and history of the Bible from the Creation to Revelation. The volume, which contains one thousand and thirty-six pages and four hundred and fifty illustrations, is replete with chronological tables and a large variety of information, arranged in analytical order so as best to assist research and contribute to a fuller understanding of the inspired word. The tables present the famous characters and events of history in a most convenient form for use in the subjective lectures of the Improvement Associations, affording at a glance the information it often requires hours of research to find.

The volume is well bound in French morocco, gilt edges, and is sold at four dollars per copy, being reduced by the agent from five dollars, the regular price. It will be mailed to any address on receipt of price and twenty-five cents for postage. Local agents are desired in various parts of the Territory, to whom liberal terms will be given. Address: R. S. Horne, Salt Lake City, U. T.

THE CONTRIBUTOR.
VOLUME SIX, 1884-5.

The publisher takes pleasure in directing attention to some of the principal features of the New Volume, which will commence with the October number and be issued on the first of each month thereafter:

THE AARONIC PRIESTHOOD,

A series of twelve papers by Bishop Orson F. Whitney. This series will be accompanied by

FOUR FULL PAGE STEEL ENGRAVINGS:

EDWARD PARTRIDGE, First Bishop of the Church. NEWEL K. WHITNEY, Bishop of Kirtland.
EDWARD HUNTER, Late Presiding Bishop. WM. B. PRESTON, Present Presiding Bishop.
Biographies of each will appear with the engravings; also biographical sketches of the late Bishops LEONARD W. HARDY and EDWIN D. WOOLLEY.

The Early Christian Church and the Apostasy,
By Elder George Reynolds.

Celestial Marriage and Congressional Enactments,
By Elder B. H. Roberts.

Martyrs of the Church,
An account of those who have suffered martyrdom in the latter days.

Dramatic Incidents of Church History,
By H. W. Naisbitt, Esq.

Australasia and the Maories,
By W. W. Day, Esq.

Scenes and Incidents in Sunny Italy,
By Dr. E. B. Ferguson.

Modern India,
By Elder William W. Willes.

Music in Utah,
Including a tribute to the memory of the late David O. Calder, by Evan Stephens, Esq.

Historical Glimpses of Colonial Times,
By Lieut. Richard W. Young.

The Carthaginians,
Including a brief life of Hannibal, by Maria M. Johnson.

Popular Science Sketches,
By Prof. James E. Talmage.

Health Series,
By Heber J. Richards, M. D.

Temple Stones,
By Theodore J. Angell.

Early Home Life in New England,
And other sketches, by Mrs. Emmeline B. Wells.

Haunts of British Poets,
Birthplace and grave of Byron; Burns' cottage and monument; home of Shakspeare.

A Historical Record,
Preserving interesting dates and events of each month, by Andrew Jenson, Esq.

A PRIZE CHRISTMAS STORY AND POEM,
For the "*Contributor Souvenir Medal*" and prizes.

Association Intelligence, Correspondence, Book Reviews, Questions and Answers and a great variety of first class reading matter.
Officers and members of Associations are urgently requested to write for the magazine.

TO AGENTS AND OFFICERS OF Y. M. M. I. A:

We have made arrangements to distribute to the libraries of the Young Men's Mutual Improvement Associations, FREE OF COST, TEN WEBSTER'S UNABRIDGED DICTIONARIES, latest edition, as described in the advertising pages of the CONTRIBUTOR, and sold at retail for $12.00 each, subject to the following conditions:
To the Y. M. M. I. A. library of each of the ten Wards having the largest paid up subscription list for VOLUME SIX, on the sixth day of April, 1885, will *be given* a WEBSTER'S UNABRIDGED DICTIONARY. *Any Ward able to supply thirty subscribers may hope to be one of the fortunate ten.* Agents in places where there are more Wards than one will always state the Ward every subscriber lives in when sending their names.

SUBSCRIPTION: Two Dollars per Annum, in Advance.

Bound Volumes, Two Dollars and a Half. Volumes bound in excellent style for subscribers at Fifty Cents each.
Ten per cent will be allowed Agents on collections made by them.
General Traveling Agent, MATTHIAS F. COWLEY.

ADDRESS.
JUNIUS F. WELLS,
CONTRIBUTOR OFFICE, MAIN ST., OPPOSITE Z. C. M. I.,

P. O. Box 305.
SALT LAKE CITY.

Remit by draft, P. O. Order or registered letter.

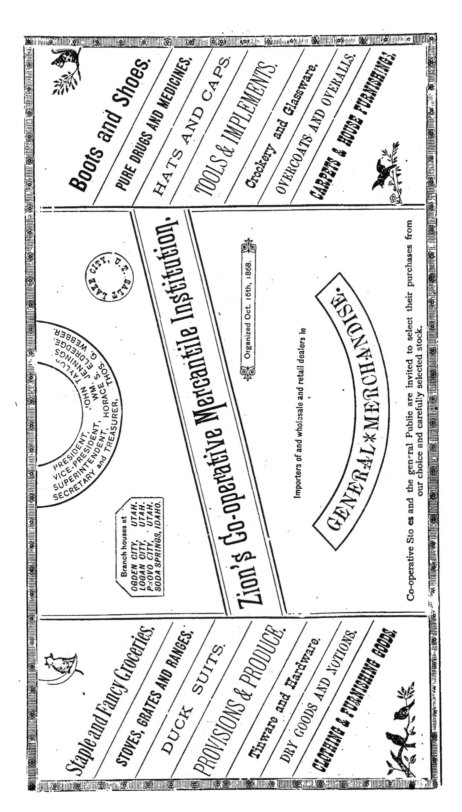

Lightning Source UK Ltd.
Milton Keynes UK
UKHW010009090219
336872UK00005B/130/P